A STORY BEHIND EVERY HYMN

52 Weeks of Inspiration, Courage and Strength

DR. LARRY FRAZIER

To Andrea,

Your life is a beautiful song!

Keep Singing!

Larry

Published by
FMC Resources, Inc
http://FaithMusicConnection.com

First Edition

ISBN: 978-0-578-63500-2

All scripture references in the devotionals are quoted from the New Revised Standard Version (NRSV) of the Bible, an English translation published in 1989 by the National Council of Churches.

Key lyrics provided are derived from each hymn. The hymns used in this book are considered public domain works.

Contents

Dedication

This book is dedicated to the memory and in honor of my mentor, Arthur T. King (1910-1968). "Prof. King" was an outstanding pianist, organist, choirmaster, symphony and opera conductor, composer and church musician. His work as Director of Music of First Presbyterian Church, Alexandria, Louisiana, inspired and prepared me for my career in music.

Acknowledgements

I am profoundly grateful to Steve Gradick, president of Gradick Communications and to Terry Lowry, my accompanist, colleague and friend, for their vision and encouragement for me to write episodes of "The Hymn of the Week." Together we came up with a format, Terry produced and recorded each episode and Steve has broadcasted the program for almost twelve years on radio station WKNG. My research into the stories behind the great hymns featured in the radio show is a core component of the 52 chapters of this book.

To Shane Fielder of Samurai Innovation, coach, consultant and fellow Christian, for helping me get Faith Music Connection online and for challenging and encouraging me to write this book.

And finally, to Mary Lynn, my dear wife, loving partner and best friend. Your faith, courage, dedication and love have encouraged and supported me in the experiences culminating in this book. Sharing life with you is an incredible joy and blessing.

Introduction

Shortly before Christmas in 2007, my wife and I were stunned at the news she had colon cancer. Surgery confirmed a diagnosis of stage-three cancer, requiring eight months of chemotherapy. The toxic treatments took a heavy toll on her, emotionally and physically, and we both had to come to grips with the possibility she might not survive.

For some time, I had been putting together "The Hymn of the Week," a 30-minute radio program featuring a traditional hymn each week. I completed the first episode about the time of her first chemotherapy treatment. I continued to write new episodes, week by week, during her increasingly difficult treatments.

We were both deeply inspired by the stories of the often-trying circumstances leading to the creation of hymns that have stood the test of time. And these stories were wonderfully therapeutic. By the time of her final treatment after which she was pronounced cancer free, I had completed well over half of the 52 episodes of "The Hymn of the Week."

From then until today, it is estimated that over 354,000 people have been supported by the "Hymn of the Week". The program is broadcasted weekly over local radio, reaching listeners in Georgia, Alabama and Tennessee. It continues to inform, comfort and inspire listeners facing significant life challenges.

This book is a weekly devotional that takes you through a collection of divinely inspired hymns by authors living their faith in a variety of challenging circumstances. Mary Lynn and I pray these hymn devotionals will comfort, inspire and strengthen you.

Each devotional contains an introduction to the story behind the creation of the hymn along with key lyrics and related scriptural references.

The book is structured so it can be used in a variety of ways. You can use this as an inspirational guide or as hymnal reference manual.

May I suggest that the simplest way is to use this as a one-year devotional book. You can also use the Alphabetical Index of Hymns to find specific hymns in which you are interested.

Regardless of how you choose to move through this book, I encourage you to read the key lyrics of each hymn. Consider how your life relates to the story that inspired the hymn. Meditate on the scriptural references. Use the included prayer to enhance your connection with God.

Second, consider memorizing some of the key lyrics of each hymn. Remember them as you go about your daily living. Praise God through the hymn. Pray as you are led by the verses of the hymn and related scripture.

A resource link is included at the end of each chapter. This link will take you to our website where you can get complete lyrics, expanded history as well as performances of each hymn. Each resource is free of charge and will allow you to hear the hymn and get more information.

Third, take good notes as you work through each devotional.

Then at the end of the book, you will be inspired by reviewing your notes and seeing the impact of the hymns in your life.

Praise God as the hymn leads you. As you consider how the hymn relates to your life, pray for forgiveness, inspiration, comfort and strength.

As you move through this book, two major themes will become obvious to you about how God moved and worked in the story and life of each hymn and author. The first is that the author was inspired by God to then write the hymn. The second is that the process of writing the hymn as a response to a tough life situation enabled God to become real and provide the comfort and strength to keep going forward.

That same God is waiting to work in your life today. Will you be open to his presence and the possibilities waiting for you?

Lastly, please be gentle with yourself as you read and study each hymn. Life is a wonderful journey if you let it be.

Wonderful journeys and stories raise questions. I welcome your questions, comments or thoughts on any of the devotionals in this book. You can email me at Larry@FaithMusicConnection.com.

KEEP SINGING!
Dr. Larry

Story # 1
All Hail the Power of Jesus' Name

Story of the Hymn

Edward Perronet's family came to England to escape religious persecution in France. Though an ordained minister, he was considered a "Non-Conformist" because of his opposition to practices of the Church of England. Despite this designation which limited his opportunities, he dutifully fulfilled a career as evangelist and pastor.

Although Perronet had his differences with religious authorities, he had no doubt of his ultimate allegiance. He wrote "All Hail the Power of Jesus' Name" during the 1770s—a period of political and religious upheaval. It was also the time of the American Revolution. This hymn is sometimes called, "The National Anthem of Christendom." It beautifully calls Christians of every age to hail the King of Kings—Jesus, who saves us by his grace.

Key Lyrics

All hail the power of Jesus' Name! Let angels prostrate fall;
Bring forth the royal diadem and crown Him Lord of all.

O that, with yonder sacred throng, we at His feet may fall,
Join in the everlasting song and crown Him Lord of all!

Devotional – Lord of All

Therefore God also highly exalted him and gave him the name that is above every name, so that at the name of Jesus every knee should bend, in heaven and on earth, and under the earth, and every tongue should confess that Jesus Christ is Lord, to the glory of God the Father. – Philippians 2:9-11

The ideal of the divine right of kings is foreign to citizens of the United States. Under this philosophy, God above, delegates supreme power to kings and queens to rule over their subjects. Every area of public and private life is under the power of the monarch. Everyone bows in the presence of this royalty. Non-conformity could bring about severe consequences.

How do you respond to these verses from Philippians? Is Jesus Christ lord and king of your life? Will you bow to him? How will you serve your king this week? What will you offer?

Edward Peronnet suggests as a first step that we join with the angels and humble ourselves at the feet of Jesus. Then he invites us to hail the king who rules forever over heaven, earth and all creation. What a powerful way to affirm our faith and allegiance by singing, "All Hail the Power of Jesus Name. And crown him, lord of all!"

Prayer
Almighty and Loving God,

Thank you for loving me not as a dictatorial king would, but as a loving Father. Thank you for your incredible love for me expressed in Jesus Christ, who through the cross and resurrection saves us all by His grace. I confess that I have not been a good subject of our Lord Jesus Christ. Forgive me for wanting to be in total control myself. Grant me grace to live as a devoted servant, with confidence and hope that Jesus is ultimately in control. Enable me to live and share this good news of unity and hope.

In Jesus' Name, Amen!

Resources - http://faithmusicconnection.com/story01

Story # 2
When I Survey the Wondrous Cross

Story of the Hymn

Isaac Watts (1674-1748), author of "When I Survey the Wondrous Cross," is universally known as the "Father of English Hymnody." Watts wrote many new paraphrases of the Psalms, including, Our God Our Help in Ages Past (Psalm 90), Jesus Shall Reign Where Ere the Sun (Psalm 72) and the Christmas hymn, Joy to the World (Psalm 98). Other Watts hymns still widely sung today include, I Sing the Mighty Power of God, Come Holy Spirit Heavenly Dove, Am I a Soldier of the Cross, Alas and Did my Savior Bleed and many others.

Isaac Watts explained his approach to writing hymns in the following quote. "Where the Psalmist describes religion by the fear of God, I have often joined faith and love to it. [Continuing] where he speaks of the pardon of sin through the mercies of God, I rather choose to mention the sacrifice of Christ, the Lamb of God. Where he promises abundance of wealth, honor and long life, I have changed some of these typical blessings for grace, glory and life eternal, which are brought to light by the gospel, and promised in the New Testament."

When I Survey the Wondrous Cross first appeared in 1707 in Watts' "Hymns and Spiritual Songs." Charles Wesley, who wrote over 6,000 hymns himself, is reported to have said he would give up all his other hymns if he could have written this one.

Key Lyrics
When I survey the wondrous cross
On which the Prince of glory died,
My richest gain I count but loss,
And pour contempt on all my pride.

Were the whole realm of nature mine,
That were a present far too small;
Love so amazing, so divine,
Demands my soul, my life, my all.

Devotional – Vain Things
May I never boast of anything except the cross of our Lord Jesus Christ, by which the world has been crucified to me, and I to the world. – Galatians 6:14

This is the key scripture on which Isaac Watts based our great hymn. Consider the second stanza.

"Forbid it, Lord, that I should boast, save in the death of Christ my God! All the vain things that charm me most, I sacrifice them to his blood."

Next, Watts compels us to look with our own eyes at our savior on the cross.

"See from His head, His hands, His feet, sorrow and love flow mingled down! Did e'er such love and sorrow meet, or thorns compose so rich a crown?"

Awesome, inspiring verses. But Watts does not stop there. Now, consider this stanza, which is rarely included in modern hymnals.

"His dying crimson, like a robe, spreads o'er His body on the tree. Then I am dead to all the globe, and all the globe is dead to me."

What "vain things charm you most?" Will you sacrifice them to His blood? In light of this hymn, how are you challenged to be crucified to the world?

Prayer
Merciful God,

Thank you for your amazing, divine love. Forgive me of the vain things that fascinate me and occupy my time. Keep my focus on your wondrous cross and enable me to serve others in your name.

Amen.

Resources - http://faithmusicconnection.com/story02

Story # 3
Nearer, My God, to Thee

Story of the Hymn

Jacob felt God's presence in a dream. Genesis 28:10-22 describes a ladder reaching from earth to heaven with God's angels ascending and descending on it. Sarah Flower Adams makes this story the basis for "Nearer my God to Thee." "There let the way appear, steps unto heaven," "all that Thou sendest me, in mercy given" and "Angels to beckon me nearer my God to thee" clearly indicate a connection with Jacob's encounter.

Key Lyrics

There let the way appear
Steps unto heaven:
All that Thou sendest me
In mercy given:
Angels to beckon me
Nearer, my God, to Thee!
(Refrain) Nearer, my God, to Thee,
Nearer to Thee!

Devotional – Ladder to Heaven

Jacob left Beer-sheba and went toward Haran. He came to a certain place and stayed there for the night, because the sun had set. Taking one of the stones of the place, he put it under his head and lay down in that place. And he dreamed that there was a ladder set up on the earth, the top of it reaching to heaven; and the angels of God were ascending and descending on it.

And the Lord stood beside him and said, "I am the Lord, the God of Abraham your father and the God of Isaac; the land on which you lie I will give to you and to your offspring. Know that I am with you wherever you go and will bring you back to this land; for I will not leave you until I have done what I have promised you."

Then Jacob woke from his sleep and said, "Surely the Lord is in this place—and I did not know it!" And he was afraid, and said, "How awesome is this place! This is none other than the house of God, and this is the gate of heaven."
– Genesis 28:10-13; 15-17

Throughout history, believers have yearned for a sense of the presence of God in their lives. The Bible is filled with stories of God's love and grace and of ordinary people called to discipleship.

Have you experienced the presence of God in your life? What experience was the most awesome? The most intimate? Where were you? Perhaps you have never felt God's presence or want to experience it anew. In Matthew 18:20, Jesus promises "where two or three are gathered together in my name, I am there among them." Find a church of caring people, sharing God's love. Worship, study and serve with them. And remember Jesus' promise in Matthew 7:7-8— "Ask, and it will be given you, search, and you will find; knock, and the door will be opened for you."

Prayer
All Present God,

Help me to sense your presence in the immensity of the universe and in the life of the smallest organisms on earth.

Your creation tells of your awesome glory. Thank you for the love you share with me through Jesus and for your spirit which draws me "nearer, my God, to Thee."

In Jesus' Name,
Amen

Resources - http://faithmusicconnection.com/story03

Story # 4
We Gather Together to Ask the Lord's Blessing

Story of the Hymn

After years of bloody religious and political conflict, Dutch forces won a decisive victory in 1597. An anonymous Dutch author wrote a hymn to thank God for the victory. Almost 300 years later, Viennese composer Eduard Kremser published the hymn together with an old Dutch folksong.

Shortly thereafter, American scholar Theodore Baker, translated the hymn into English and brought it to the United States. It has become a favorite hymn of thanksgiving.

Key Lyrics

We gather together to ask the Lord's blessing;
Beside us to guide us, our God with us joining,
Ordaining, maintaining His kingdom divine.
Thy name be ever praised! O Lord, make us free!

Devotional – Humble Thanksgiving

Make a joyful noise to the Lord, all the earth. Worship the Lord with gladness; come into his presence with singing. Know that the Lord is God. It is he that made us, and we are his. We are his people and the sheep of his pasture. Enter his gates with thanksgiving and his courts with praise. Give thanks to him; bless his name. For the Lord is good; his steadfast love endures forever and his faithfulness to all generations.
– Psalm 100

No one is immune from the ravages of life—natural disasters, war, disease, death.

In responding to this reality, hymn writers, through the ages, have encouraged a spirit of humble thankfulness for life's blessings. Both the author of our hymn and the author of Psalm 100 write from the perspective of "we" not "I." Perhaps this is a key of both thankfulness and thanksgiving.

Make a list of some things for which you are thankful. Try to list at least 24. (You might list blessings beginning with each letter of the alphabet.) Go back through your list. How many involve only you? Are you surprised?

We celebrate happy events—birthdays, anniversaries, victories to name a few—together. Conversely, tragedies also bring us together. Our anonymous hymn writer was grateful for the victory but certainly also aware of the tragic costs of the war it ended. Yet, the first line is a call to prayer— "We gather together to ask the Lord's blessing." A spirit of thankfulness pervades the entire hymn, but within a framework of service in God's divine kingdom.

Christians regularly gather together for worship. Collectively, we praise God, express thanks for our blessings, confess our sins. We sing hymns. Worship inspires and invigorates the sharing of our faith as we serve others.

Prayer
Bountiful God,

Thank you for the many blessings I enjoy. Thank you for being with me in good and difficult times. Please forgive me for taking blessings for granted and for forgetting how many of these are possible only through others. Give me a thankful heart and a discerning mind to be your disciple.

In Jesus' Name,
Amen

Resources **-** http://faithmusicconnection.com/story04

Story # 5

Blessed Assurance, Jesus is Mine!

Story of the Hymn

Phoebe Knapp composed the music for over 500 gospel songs, but it is for her tune "Assurance" that she is remembered today. Fanny Crosby, in describing the circumstances of how she wrote Blessed Assurance, is reported to have said that her friend, Mrs. Joseph F. Knapp, composed a melody and after playing it over for her two or three times on the piano, asked what the music said. She answered, "it says Blessed Assurance, Jesus is Mine!" and quickly wrote out all three stanzas with refrain. The women remained close friends until Phoebe Knapp's death in 1908.

Key Lyrics

Blessed assurance, Jesus is mine!
O what a foretaste of glory divine!
Heir of Salvation, purchase of God,
Born of his spirit, washed in his blood.
This is my story, this is my song
Praising my savior all the day long

Devotional – Focused on Blessings

...I know the one in whom I have put my trust, and I am sure that he is able to guard until that day what I have entrusted to him. – 2 Timothy 1:12

Though blind from the age of two weeks, Fanny Crosby seems to have never considered blindness to be a handicap. Even as a young child, she was able to play outdoors with other children, running, jumping and climbing trees. She excelled as a student and later as a member of the faculty of The New

York Institute for the Blind. Combining her poetic and scholarly gifts, she wrote over 8,000 hymns before her death at age 95, in 1915.

No hymnwriter has written more. The next most prolific author, Charles Wesley, wrote only 6,500, 1,500 fewer!

Fanny Crosby's life was hugely successful, but she also endured much grief. Her only child died in infancy, and her husband of 44 years died when she was 82. Her close friend, Phoebe Knapp, who wrote the music for Crosby's, "Blessed Assurance," died six years later.

Fanny Crosby provides several keys to successfully pursuing happiness and to glorifying and enjoying God in her remarkable poetic output. Consider her first childhood poem.

Oh, what a happy soul I am!
Although I cannot see,
I am resolved that in this world
Contented I will be.
How many blessings I enjoy
That other people don't!
To weep and sigh because I'm blind,
I cannot, nor I won't!

First, she clearly had an attitude of determination to be happy and content. Second, she focused intently on her blessings rather than her difficulties. Third, though she was keenly aware of her blindness, she would not let that get her down.

Finally, she declares faith in God as the key to happiness in her beloved hymn, "Blessed Assurance, Jesus is Mine.

Blessed assurance, Jesus is mine!
O what a foretaste of glory divine!
Heir of Salvation, purchase of God,
Born of his spirit, washed in his blood.

Prayer
Dear God,

Thank you for the life of Fanny Crosby and for her great hymn, "Blessed Assurance, Jesus is Mine!" Renew my spirit and grant me the confidence of these beautiful verses so that I may praise my savior "all the day long."

In Jesus' Name,
Amen

Resources **-** http://faithmusicconnection.com/story05

Story # 6
Abide with Me

Story of the Hymn

For centuries, the hardy residents of Lower Brixham, Devonshire, England, made their living from the wilderness of the sea. They were keenly aware of the fragileness of life and the possibility of unexpected death and heartache. Indeed, the bells of the small Anglican church located there routinely rang in commemoration of another passing.

In 1824, the Church of England sent a young man from Scotland to be the pastor of All Saints Church in Lower Brixham. Henry Francis Lyte had spent most of his childhood in orphanages. He was a scholarly man of keen intellect and rather fragile health, continually bothered by asthma—a rather unlikely choice for the hearty parishioners.

But he was also a compassionate man, and he was keenly devoted to his duties as pastor. Over the years he found time to write numerous hymns.

In 1847, he was stricken with tuberculosis. Certainly, aware that his earthly life was coming to an end, he wrote "Abide with Me" just three weeks before his death. Today, the bells of All Saints Church continue to daily ring out the melody universally paired with this hymn. What a resounding testament to Henry Francis Lyte and a life well-lived!

Key Lyrics

Abide with me; fast falls the eventide;
The darkness deepens; Lord with me abide.

When other helpers fail and comforts flee,
Help of the helpless, O abide with me.

Devotional – Stay with Me

As they came near the village to which they were going, he (the resurrected Jesus) walked ahead as if he were going on. But they urged him strongly, saying, "Stay with us, because it is almost evening and the day is now nearly over." So, he went in to stay with them. When he was at the table with them, he took bread, blessed and broke it, and gave it to them. Then their eyes were opened, and they recognized him; and he vanished from their sight. They said to each other, "Were not our hearts burning within us while he was talking to us on the road, while he was opening the scriptures to us?"
– Luke 24:28-32

Henry Francis Lyte's poem "Ere the Night Fall" gives insight into his life and ministry and states his dying wish as follows.

"Why do I sigh to find Life's evening shadows gathering round my way, the keen eye dimming, and the buoyant mind unhinging day by day? I want not vulgar fame—I seek not to survive in brass and stone! Hearts may not kindle when they hear my name, Nor tears my value own: But might I leave behind some blessing for my fellows, some fair trust To guide, to cheer, to elevate my kind, when I am in the dust; Might verse of mine inspire One virtuous aim, One high resolve impart, Light in one drooping soul a hallowed fire, Or bind one broken heart; Death would be sweeter then, more calm my slumber 'neath the silent sod—Might I thus live to bless my fellow-men, Or glorify my God! O Thou whose touch can lend life to the dead, thy quickening grace supply, And grant me, swanlike, my last breath to spend in song that may not die!" This dying wish is indeed fulfilled in "Abide with Me."

From the website of All Saints Church, Brixham, is a simple, inspiring message reminding us to be attentive to the needs of all those living among us who need help.

"A Thought

Living where we do, we often hear the maroons go up and there will be a mad dash to launch the lifeboat from the harbour. This means that somebody somewhere needs help. You may not hear them, but you will certainly hear the sirens from police, ambulance or fire service. When you do, just stop and offer a prayer. Offer one for those who need emergency help, one for the brave rescuers and one for whoever it was who made the call. It will only take a few seconds, but you will have done your bit for all of them."

Prayer
Dear Lord,

Abide with me and enable me to "do my bit" for all who need help. Amen!

Resources **-** http://faithmusicconnection.com/story06

Story # 7
Precious Lord, Take My Hand

Story of the Hymn
It was the "roaring 20's." A man known as "Barrel House Tom" established a career as a blues pianist, first in Atlanta, and then in Chicago. He was from Villa Rica, Georgia, a town closer to Alabama than to Atlanta. His father was a poor sharecropper and itinerant preacher, so his earliest musical experience was in the church.

"Barrel House Tom" performed as piano accompanist for singers such as Mahalia Jackson, Clara Ward and Della Reese. He was such an accomplished blues pianist that Ma Rainey personally chose him to lead her "Wild Cats Jazz Band."

Then, tragedy struck. His wife died in childbirth, and the next day his infant son also died. Thomas A. Dorsey poured out his grief and cried out in faith to his lord and savior in a great hymn. This hymn, "Precious Lord, Take my Hand," has comforted many through the years and was a favorite of Dr. Martin Luther King, Jr.

Key Lyrics
Precious Lord, take my hand,
Lead me on, let me stand,
I am tired, I am weak, I am worn;
Through the storm, through the night,
Lead me on to the light

Refrain: Take my hand, precious Lord,
Lead me home.

Devotional – Almost Gone

"Come to me, all you that are weary and carrying heavy burdens, and I will give you rest. Take my yoke upon you and learn from me; for I am gentle and humble of heart, and you will find rest for your souls. For my yoke is easy, and my burden is light." – Matthew 11:28-30

Here is the inspiring story of our hymn as told in his own words by Thomas A. Dorsey.

"Blues, jazz, the Gospel. I want to talk about the gospel songs. After going that field, I went out to go to St. Louis one morning to work a revival. I left my wife asleep in bed. Got in my car, and I went along. She was going to become a mother, and I was anticipating a great happiness and great joy on my return.

When I got to St. Louie and about the second night in the meeting, a telegram boy came and brought me a telegram. I opened it and read, "your wife just died; come home." I couldn't finish the meeting.

Finally, I got home to Chicago the next morning. And it was so; I found it all true. They never moved the body. And that chilled me, killed me off! I wanted to go back to blues.

But, after putting my wife away and the baby in the same casket, I went to old Poro College, in the music room. There, crying, I just 'brosed' (browsed?) over the keys. And seemingly the words, like drops of water from a crevice of a rock above, seemed to drop in line. 'Precious Lord, Take my Hand. Lead me on, let me stand. I'm tired, I'm weak, I'm worn. Through the storm, through the night, lead me on to the light. Take my hand, precious Lord, and lead me home.'"

Prayer

When my way grows drear,
Precious Lord, linger near,
When my life is almost gone,
Hear my cry, hear my call,
Hold my hand lest I fall:

Refrain: Take my hand, precious Lord,
Lead me home.

Amen.

Resources **–** http://faithmusicconnection.com/story07

Story # 8
Rock of Ages

Story of the Hymn

In Somerset, in Southwest England, there is a rugged area of craggy, limestone cliffs rising to heights of up to 250 feet, backed by steep valleys or hollows. Natural erosion from rainfall has created many caves and crevices in these outcroppings. Within this area lies Burrington Combe, dramatically marked by a tall cliff with deep crevices splitting it down the middle. Burrington Combe also contains the large rock popularly known as the "Rock of Ages." Anglican pastor Augustus Montague Toplady (1740-1778) served several churches located nearby.

He is reputed to have taken refuge under this rock during a sudden thunderstorm, inspiring the hymn. As appealing as this story may be, most authorities agree it was probably written several years later, in London. Toplady had left the Anglican Church and moved there to preach at a French Calvinist church.

Whatever the inspiration, *Rock of Ages* has provided special comfort to those facing death or tragic circumstances.

Key Lyrics

Rock of Ages, Cleft for me,
Let me hide myself in Thee;
Let the water and the blood,
From Thy wounded side which flowed,
Be of sin the double cure;
Cleanse me from its guilt and power.

Devotional – Hide and Seek

When I thought, "My foot is slipping," your steadfast love, O Lord, held me up. When the cares of my heart are many, your consolations cheer my soul. –Psalm 94:18-19

O come, let us sing to the Lord; let us make a joyful noise to the rock of our salvation! –Psalm 95:1

One of the soldiers pierced his side with a spear, and at once blood and water came out. – John 19:34

This is the one who came by water and blood, Jesus Christ, not with water only but with the water and the blood. And the Spirit is the one that testifies, for the Spirit is the truth…And this is the testimony: God gave us eternal life, and this life is in his Son. –1 John 5:6, 11

And all drank the same spiritual drink. For they drank from the spiritual rock that followed them, and the rock was Christ. –1 Corinthians 10:4

Like the scripture above, "Rock of Ages" is rich with language amplifying the central truth of Christianity. God loves us so much that he gives us eternal life through Jesus Christ to all who believe. God's sacrificial love involves blood, water, excruciatingly painful death on a cross, resurrection and grace. The rock core of this love is Jesus Christ, wholly God and fully human, yet without sin. God's Spirit testifies of God's love in Jesus Christ and empowers us to believe.

Do you remember playing "Hide and Seek?" It was fun to find a hiding place that took awhile to be discovered. And it was also fun to quickly discover the hiding place of the other player. What was not so much fun was to hide so well that the other player could not find you within a reasonable time.

In our hymn, Augustus Toplady twice asks Jesus, the Rock of Ages, "Let me hide myself in Thee." First, at the beginning of the first stanza and second, at the end of the final stanza.

What would it be like to hide yourself in Jesus? Could you be recognized? If so, how would you be different?

Prayer
Rock of Ages,

Nothing I do, nor my best intentions can overcome my sin. Thank you for your sacrificial love in Jesus Christ. Please forgive me and cleanse me from the guilt and power of sin in my life, and "let me hide myself in Thee."

In Jesus' Name,
Amen

Resources **-** http://faithmusicconnection.com/story08

Story # 9
The Church's One Foundation

Story of the Hymn

The Church's One Foundation is the most famous of the many hymns written by Samuel John Stone. He was born in 1839 at Whitmore, Strattfordshire, England, the son of An Anglican minister. After completing his baccalaureate degree from Pembroke College, Oxford, in 1862, He was ordained in the Church of England.

Stone served as curate of Windsor from 1862 to 1870. Shortly after competing graduate studies at Pembroke in 1872, he was appointed vicar of St. Paul's Haggerston, located in a poor section of London. He worked tirelessly for the benefit of the people of his parish and became known as "the poor man's pastor."

Also, a man of letters, Samuel J. Stone published in 1866, *Lyra Fidelium*, a cycle of twelve hymns on the twelve articles of the Apostle's Creed. The ninth article, "I believe in the holy catholic church" —referring to the church universal—was the basis for *The Church's One Foundation.* This hymn beautifully amplifies the communion of all believers in relationship with Jesus Christ as head of the church.

Key Lyrics

The Church's One Foundation
Is Jesus Christ her Lord,
She is His new creation
By water and the Word.
From heaven He came and sought her

To be His holy bride;
With His own blood he bought her,
And for her life He died.

Devotional – Eyes of the Heart

I pray that the God of our Lord Jesus Christ, the Father of glory, may give you a spirit of wisdom and revelation as you come to know him, so that, with the eyes of your heart enlightened, you may know what is the hope to which he has called you, what are the riches of his glorious inheritance among the saints, and what is the immeasurable greatness of his power for us who believe, according to the working of his great power.

God put this power to work in Christ when he raised him from the dead and seated him at his right hand in the heavenly places, far above all rule and authority and power and dominion, and above every name that is named, not only in this age but also in the age to come. And he has put all things under his feet and has made him head over all things for the church, which is his body, the fullness of him who fills all in all. – Ephesians 1:17-23

18th-century Scottish poet Robert Burns mused that seeing ourselves as others see us would free us from many a blunder. In the above passage from Ephesians, St. Paul seems to be praying that we see ourselves as God sees us—as we really are. Both individually, and collectively, as members of the institutional church, we are flawed and sinful. Yet God loves us as we are and calls us and the church to love God totally and our neighbors as ourselves.

Another hymn by Samuel J. Stone, his personal favorite, is worthy of our meditation.

Weary of earth, and laden with my sin,
I look at Heav'n and long to enter in,
But there no evil thing may find a home:
And yet I hear a voice that bids me "Come."

It is the voice of Jesus that I hear;
His are the hands stretched out to draw me near,
And His blood that can for all atone,
And set me faultless there before the throne.

Yea, Thou wilt answer for me, righteous Lord;
Thine all the merits, mine the great reward;
Thine the sharp thorns, and mine the golden crown;
Mine the life won, and Thine the life laid down.

Naught can I bring, dear Lord, for all I owe,
Yet let my full heart what it can bestow;
Like Mary's gift, let my devotion prove,
Forgiven greatly, how greatly I love.

Prayer
Father of Glory,

Thank you for loving me unconditionally through Jesus. Give me the eyes of an enlightened heart and the grace to be a caring person, sharing your love.

In Jesus' Name,
Amen

Resources – http://faithmusicconnection.com/story09

Story # 10
Amazing Grace

Story of the Hymn

John Newton, (1725-1807) author of "Amazing Grace, was the son of a slave-ship captain. His mother died when he was six, and his father ended his formal schooling after only two years. Captain Newton treated his son harshly, keeping him continually at sea from age 11. He showed him no favors and left him to fend for himself among the sea-hardened sailors among whom he lived and toiled. Years later, Newton wrote this about himself as a young sailor, "I was capable of anything; I had not the least fear of God before my eyes, nor (so far as I remember) the least sensibility of conscience."

Ironically, John Newton eventually captained a slave-trading ship himself. During a particularly severe storm at sea, he had a spiritual awakening while praying for God's mercy. Newton ended his seafaring career in 1754 and became one of the chief advocates for the abolishment of slave trading in the British Isles.

Newton taught himself to read Greek and Hebrew, and his faith and understanding grew. In 1764, he was ordained in the Church of England, and was made pastor of the parish at Olney. A compassionate and loving pastor, he became popular with his parishioners, including many of the poor and illiterate who toiled as lace makers.

It was at Olney that Newton became pastor to the troubled poet William Cowper, who suffered continual bouts of severe depression. To help his friend, Newton suggested that he and

Cowper collaborate in writing a series of hymns to accompany his sermons. Cowper was able to complete only 67 hymns before becoming completely mentally incapacitated, but Newton continued at the rate of one hymn per week until a total of 348 hymns had been written for the collection, known as the "Olney Hymns." "Amazing Grace" first appeared in this collection, in 1779.

Newton wrote "Amazing Grace" to accompany a New Year's sermon based on 1 Chronicles 17:16. Then King David went in and sat before the Lord, and said, "Who am I, O Lord God, and what is my house, that you have brought me thus far?" The final phrase of this verse is clearly reflected in the third stanza of this great hymn—"Tis Grace has brought me safe thus far, and Grace will lead me home!"

"Amazing Grace" is perhaps the most popular hymn of all time. It appears in almost every modern hymnal and has been translated into numerous languages. Though its tune is known throughout the world, performed by professional opera singers, country music stars, folk singers and bagpipers, sung in churches from the humblest country church to the greatest cathedrals, the composer is unknown.

Key Lyrics

Amazing grace! How sweet the sound
That saved a wretch like me!
I once was lost, but now am found;
Was blind, but now I see.

Through many dangers, toils and snares,
I have already come;
'Tis grace hath brought me safe thus far,
And grace will lead me home.

Devotional – Amazing Grace

Then King David went in and sat before the Lord, and said, "Who am I, O Lord God, and what is my house, that you have brought me thus far?" –1 Chronicles 17:16

Because his conversion to Christianity was so dramatic, and because he was such a prolific writer, John Newton continues to be our pastor today. On controversy and religious extremism, he wrote, "If our zeal is embittered by expressions of anger, invective, or scorn, we may think we are doing service to the cause of truth, when in reality we shall only bring it into discredit."

On the love of God and our response he writes,

Let us love and sing and wonder,
Let us praise the Savior's Name!
When through grace in Christ our trust is,
Justice smiles and asks no more:
He who washed us with his blood
Has secured our way to God.

Prayer (Benediction by John Newton – 1779)

May the grace of Christ our Savior
And the Father's boundless love
With the Holy Spirit's favor,
Rest upon us from above.

Amen.

Resources - http://faithmusicconnection.com/story10

Story # 11
All Creatures of Our God and King

Story of the Hymn

St. Francis of Assisi wrote "Cantico di frate sole" (Hymn of Brother Sun) shortly before his death in 1226. This poem, considered to be the first literary work written in Italian, is a statement of faith and values lived by this great Christian saint. Born into a family of wealth and privilege, with handsome features and easy manner.

Francis was a favorite among the elite, enjoying a life of luxury and ease, until an encounter with a lowly beggar and revelations received in dreams following serious illness brought about a complete change in his life as he sought to live like Jesus Christ.

He embraced poverty and shared the love of God for everyone—especially, the most disadvantaged—and an appreciation for all of God's creation, including animals and nature as well as other people.

His conversion was sincere and genuine, and he attracted many followers during his lifetime. So profound was Francis' influence that even today, Franciscans throughout the world continue to seek to show the love of Jesus Christ through embracing vows of poverty and serving others in a spirit of kindness and humility.

William H. Draper, an Anglican priest, translated Francis' poem into English for use at a children's Whitsuntide (or Pentecost) festival in Leeds, England; the resulting All

Creatures of our God and King first appeared in the Public School Hymn Book, in 1919.

Key Lyrics

All creatures of our God and King,
Lift up your voice and with us sing,
Alleluia! Alleluia!
Thou burning sun with golden beam,
Thou silver moon with softer gleam!
Refrain —
O praise Him!
O praise Him! Alleluia! Alleluia! Alleluia!

Devotional – A Different Footprint

All your works shall give thanks to you, O Lord, and all your faithful shall bless you. They shall speak of the glory of your kingdom, and tell of your power, to make known to all people your mighty deeds, and the glorious splendor of your kingdom. Your kingdom is an everlasting kingdom, and your dominion endures throughout all generations.

The Lord is faithful in all his words, and gracious in all his deeds. The Lord upholds all who are falling and raises up all who are bowed down.

The eyes of all look to you, and you give them their food in due season. You open your hand, satisfying the desire of every living thing.

The Lord is just in all his ways, and kind in all his doings. The Lord is near to all who call on him, to all who call on him in truth. He fulfills the desire of all who fear him; he also hears their cry and saves them. The Lord watches over all who love

him, but all the wicked he will destroy. My mouth will speak the praise of the Lord, and all flesh will bless his holy name forever and ever.
- Psalm 145:10-21

Among numerous allusions to scripture from both Old and New Testaments, perhaps none in in closer harmony to the spirit of *All Creatures of Our God and King* than is this passage from Psalm 145. St. Francis of Assisi is remembered for his love of animals and a deep appreciation for the interdependence of all living things, coexisting under the care of a loving and awesome Creator/God.

In our 21st-century world marred by hurricanes, earthquakes, fire and famine and irresponsible use of earth's resources and conflict between nations, political discord and personal rancor all around, it seems almost naïve to sing such a hymn. Our carbon footprint threatens the quality of life of all on our planet. What can I do in the face of such a climate?

Perhaps we can re-discover another footprint, one that has inspired believers for eight centuries. Francis' footprint of repudiation of material wealth and privilege for a life devoted to love and service remains. Perhaps in following this footprint we can more truthfully and joyfully sing "All Creatures of Our God and King."

Prayer
God of all Creation,

Thank you for your loving care for me and for all living things. I confess that I have not been a good steward of the blessings of your creation. Forgive me. Open my heart. Enable me to show love where there is hatred and make me an instrument of your peace.

In Jesus' Name,
Amen

Resources - http://faithmusicconnection.com/story11

Story # 12
Now Thank We All Our God

Story of the Hymn

The Thirty Years' War, lasting from 1618 to 1648, was a series of wars over political and religious conflicts involving most of Europe. Battlefronts were concentrated in the German provinces of Silesia and Saxony. The destruction of war accompanied by pillage, rape, injustice and lawlessness was almost unbearable to the citizens of Eilenburg, a walled city near the modern city of Leipzig, Germany. Overwhelmed by many refugees, a shortage of food and housing and poor sanitation, disease and plague claimed more lives than war. It was a time that tested the character and faith of even the strongest.

Martin Rinkart, a Lutheran minister educated at St. Thomas' School in Leipzig, returned to his native Eilenburg in 1618. There, he served as pastor of one of four Lutheran churches for over thirty years until his death in 1649. His pastorate encompassed the full duration of The Thirty Years' War. During one of the darkest periods of the war, plague claimed hundreds of victims per week in Eilenburg. Soon, Rinkart was the only pastor remaining, the others having joined the thousands who died.

One day, just before sitting down to a meal with his family, Martin Rinkart looked out his window as carts carrying the bodies of the dead moved slowly through the streets of Eilenburg, Instead of despairing, he was moved to write "Nun danket alle Gott" ("Now Thank We All Our God"). He intended the first two stanzas as a prayer before meals with his family and the third as a personal statement of thanksgiving and faith in an all-powerful God. Written in 1636, it was first published about ten years later in Berlin. Catherine Winkworth, nineteenth-century English scholar, translated the hymn into English and included it in her collection, "Lyrica Germanica," published in 1858.

Key Lyrics

Now thank we all our God With heart and hands and voices
Who wondrous things hath done, In whom this world rejoices;
Who, from our mothers' arms, Hath blessed us on our way
With countless gifts of love, And still is ours today.

Devotional – Spirit of Thankfulness

As you therefore have received Christ Jesus the Lord, continue to live your lives in him, rooted and built up in him and established in the faith, just as you were taught, abounding in thanksgiving. —Colossians 2:6-7

Rejoice in the Lord always; again, I will say, Rejoice. Let your gentleness be known to everyone. The Lord is near. Do not worry about anything, but in everything by prayer and supplication with thanksgiving let your requests be made known to God. And the peace of God, which surpasses all understanding, will guard your hearts and your minds in Christ Jesus. –Philippians 4:4-7

A spirit of thankfulness or a grateful heart is encouraged in Scripture, but it is a quality that seems to be as difficult to cultivate today as it must have been when Martin Rinkart wrote, *Now Thank We All Our God.* A great business baron is reputed to have answered the question, "How much money is enough?" with the statement, "...One more dollar than I have."

Expanding personal initiative brought about by great advances in science and medicine and increases in knowledge and in communications seem to insulate us from the idea of being grateful to an omnipotent God who provides sustenance for all our needs. In contrast, many people in the world live in oppression, poverty, hunger and inadequate housing.

Perhaps their suffering is not far removed from that endured by the people of Eilenburg in the seventeenth century or from others throughout history. Surely, their sturdy faith, affirmed in "Now Thank We All Our God," is an example for us today. And, not just an example—for we can sing it!

Prayer
Gracious Lord,

I confess that I get too caught up in the complexities of daily life. I worry about money and the challenges of war and terrorism, poverty and hunger. Keep my eyes open to these problems but help me to remember to first come to you in prayer and supplication and with a spirit of thankfulness, so that I may live and serve you in perfect peace.

In Jesus' Name,
Amen

Resources - http://faithmusicconnection.com/story12

Story # 13
Be Thou My Vision

Story of the Hymn

The three-hundred years following the missionary visits of St. Patrick in the early 5th century was a time of great increase of the Christian faith in Ireland. The Irish eagerly embraced the good news of the gospel of Christ; many churches were built, and Christian faith and worship soon replaced the pagan practices and cultural leadership of the Druid priests.

During this period, Irish Christians not only shared their faith on their island homeland but also began to send missionaries throughout the world.

The old Irish poem, *Rop tu ma wahleur (phonetic pronunciation)* "Be Thou My Vision" comes from this time of spiritual awakening. Although some scholars attribute the poem to Dallan Forgail, of the sixth century or even to St. Patrick himself, the true author is unknown.

The poem follows the form of the Celtic "lorica"—a prayer for spiritual and physical protection. It is known to us today because of the interest in Gaelic culture and the efforts of two British scholars born in the late 19th century.

Translated by Mary E. Byrne, it was published in 1905 in Dublin in the Journal of the School of Irish Learning; Eleanor H. Hull, founder of the Irish Literary Society in London, arranged the translated text into verses published in 1912, in *Poem-book of the Gael.*

The translated verses portray a deep devotion and depth of faith with metaphoric references to God as Vision, Wisdom, Father, Treasure, Heart, Ruler, Inheritance which invoke a spirit of reverence in us today.

Key Lyrics
Be Thou my Vision, O Lord of my heart;
Naught be all else to me, save that Thou art.
Thou my best Thought, by day or by night,
Waking or sleeping, Thy presence my light.

Devotional – Presence of God
But blessed are our eyes, for they see, and your ears, for they hear. Truly I tell you, many prophets and righteous people longed to see what you see, but did not see it, and to hear what you hear, but did not hear it. –Matthew 13:16-17

The approximate 2,000 years from the life of Jesus Christ on earth to today are marked with countless stories of the lives of believers and their expressions of faith, which have connected and inspired Christians through the centuries. This great connection of believers is described in ancient creeds as "The Communion of the Saints."

Among the gifts of Irish Christians to the practice of our faith is a Celtic awareness and appreciation of the presence of God in all things created. Although this spirituality was often at odds with orthodox Christian practice, it continues to be a part of what has become a great tradition of contemplative meditation, prayer and devotion.

Where and when do you sense the presence of God? In Prayer? Worship? Communion? In service to others? When you read the Bible? Are you in awe of God when you view a mountain scene or waves crashing on a beach? Or, perhaps you do not sense God's presence at all?

Both verse and tune of "Be Thou My Vision beautifully express faith in a God of ultimate power, wisdom and goodness. This hymn also shares the longing of the believer for true communion with God encompassing past, present and future, culminating in the joys of heaven. This is a prayer to which most of us can relate. When coupled with the ancient Celtic tune, "Slane," it can resonate in our voices as well as in our hearts...God be in our singing!

Prayer
Awesome God,

Thank you for the gift of a connection with believers from ancient Ireland. May their prayer become mine—God be in my vision, my wisdom, my treasure. God be in my heart, the ruler of my life, and God be my inheritance of all that is good, right and true!

In Jesus Name,
Amen

Resources - http://faithmusicconnection.com/story13

Story # 14
Shall We Gather at the River

Story of the Hymn
Robert Lowry was pastor of a large church in Brooklyn when he wrote *Shall We Gather at the River* during an extremely hot July day in 1864. Suffering from symptoms of heat exhaustion and the burden of ministering to the many victims of a typhoid epidemic sweeping the city, he had an apocalyptic vision of the gathering of the saints at the heavenly river flowing in a crystal-clear stream beneath the throne of God.

As he contemplated the scene, both the words and the music of the hymn seemed to flow into his consciousness, proceeding from the question, "Shall we gather?" to the emphatic answer of the refrain, "Yes, we'll gather."

Invigorated by this burst of inspiration, he quickly moved to the parlor organ in his home, where he played and sang the first stanza. He then quickly wrote out the entire hymn, words and music.

Key Lyrics
Shall we gather at the river,
Where bright angel feet have trod,
With its crystal tide forever
Flowing by the throne of God?

Yes, we'll gather at the river,
The beautiful, the beautiful river;
Gather with the saints at the river
That flows by the throne of God.

Devotional – Group Connection

"Then the angel showed me the river of life, bright as crystal, flowing from the throne of God and of the Lamb through the middle street of the city. Let anyone who wishes take the water of life as a gift...The grace of the Lord Jesus be with all the saints."–Revelation 22:1-2a; 17b; 21

Groups of all kinds value meeting together as a means of building identity, unity, enthusiasm and support. Political groups meet to increase campaign contributions and to motivate their members to get out the vote for their candidates. Fitness trainers form groups of those interested in building strength, flexibility and aerobic fitness knowing that success is often greater for those working together to achieve challenging goals. Stadiums, coliseums and arenas across the world are filled with thousands of sports fans eagerly cheering on their team to victory.

One of the great civic clubs, Rotary International, places a strong emphasis on regular attendance at weekly meetings. One of its central principles stresses meeting together as an opportunity for service.

To what groups do you belong? Are you active in any groups of Christian believers? How do you benefit from membership? What do you do for the success of the group? What would your life be like without these groups.?

From the earliest establishment of Christianity, Christians have regularly met together in groups large and small to share the faith and for worship, prayer, education and study, fellowship and in service to others. Jesus is quoted in Matthew 18:20, "For where two or three are gathered in my name, I am there among them." From large crowds at Christmas and Easter to the smallest of prayer groups, Christians feel and are motivated by this presence and power.

From the happiness of weddings to the sadness of funerals and the communion felt in the sharing of the Lord's Supper, Christians celebrate their faith and sense of connection to each other and to Christ. Music, unique and mystical in its power to connect, is usually a part of these gatherings.

Shall We Gather at the River affirms a faith in an ultimate gathering and reunion of all believers.

Prayer
Great God of Heaven,

Thank you for calling me to live and serve with other believers in service of your kingdom. I look forward to the great gathering of all believers at the river of the water of life, flowing from your throne. Please keep me thirsty for this water.

In the Name of Jesus Christ,
Amen

Resources - http://faithmusicconnection.com/story14

Story # 15
Holy, Holy, Holy!

Story of the Hymn

Reginald Heber (1783-1826), the pastor of a small Anglican church and a scholar of ancient Greek and Hebrew and Christian doctrine, combined his scholarly and liturgical knowledge with his considerable poetic gifts in writing his greatest hymn— "Holy, Holy, Holy!"

Heber wrote the hymn in the rather unusual meter of 12. 12. 12. 10. Composer John Bacchus Dykes recognized the beauty of these verses and composed a tune for them, which he aptly named, "Nicaea." (Nicaea was the place where the principle doctrines of Christianity were compiled and ratified into the Nicene Creed in the fourth century.)

Heber forged poetic references to the Nicene Creed and the doctrine of the Trinity, the sovereignty of God, Psalm 19 and to the books of Isaiah and Revelation to create a hymn which the great poet Alfred Lord Tennyson is said to have considered one of the finest hymns ever written.

Key Lyrics

Holy, holy, holy! Lord God Almighty!
All thy works shall praise thy name in earth and sky and sea;
Holy, holy, holy! merciful and mighty;
God in three persons, blessed Trinity!

Devotional – Song Rising

Holy, holy, holy is the Lord of Hosts; the whole earth is full of his glory. –Isaiah 6:3

Holy, holy, holy is the Lord Almighty, who was and is and is to come. –Revelation 4:8

The heavens are telling the glory of God; and the firmament proclaims his handiwork. Day to day pours forth speech, and night to night declares knowledge. There is no speech, nor are there words; their voice is not heard; Yet their voice goes out through all the earth, and their words to the end of the world. In the heavens he has set a tent for the sun. –Psalm 19:1-5

The concept of God as being perfect in goodness and righteousness and worthy of complete devotion is a central theme of the Bible.

From the earliest days of Christianity, the Sanctus (the Latin word which translates as "holy") has been a part of the liturgy of the Mass. Today, every Mass of the Catholic Church throughout the world includes the Sanctus sung or spoken in the vernacular.

Because of its universal use in the Mass, "Holy, holy, holy" is the hymn text that is probably sung or spoken more often than any other.

What does "holy" mean to you? What in your life is holy? How do you act or respond to what is holy? Why do you think the title and first line of this hymn state the word "holy" three times instead of just once?

A great hymn has a unique ability to inspire us today. Hymns are the poetic testimonies of people throughout history who have lived out their faith in good times and bad. Together with scripture, hymns invite us to discover anew the love of God and to share this love in our worship with other believers and in lives of true discipleship until we too, may "cast down our golden crowns around the glassy sea before the "Holy Lord God Almighty!" The beautiful poetry of Reginald Heber's hymn is a sort of paraphrase of the statement of faith crafted by those early church leaders who met at Nicaea, that, when coupled with John Dykes' wonderful tune, resonates within our hearts.

Prayer
Holy God,

You, alone, are holy. I love to worship you, praising you in prayer and in hymns of praise. Bless my life so that it may be like a song rising to Thee.

In Jesus' Holy Name,
Amen

Resources - http://faithmusicconnection.com/story15

Story # 16
For the Beauty of the Earth

Story of the Hymn

"For the Beauty of the Earth," by Folliott Sandford Pierpont, was first published in 1864, in a collection of communion hymns entitled "Lyra Eucharistica." Pierpont, born in Bath, Somerset, England, in 1835, was an honor graduate of Queens College, Cambridge, where he excelled as a student of the classics. After a short stint as headmaster and teacher of classics at Somersetshire College, he devoted his creative energy to writing, producing over seven volumes of hymns and sacred poems.

Though widely traveled, Pierpoint lived most of his life in Bath; his life-long appreciation of nature and the beautiful countryside of southwest England crowned in the purple of violets and the pale-yellow primrose of Spring is reflected in his most famous hymn.

A devout lay member of the Anglican Church, he was also committed to the ideals of the Oxford or Tracterian Movement, which sought to establish a more formal liturgy with communion as a central part of the service of worship in which hymns reflect more the collective voice of the people instead of the individual, personal experience emphasized in evangelical hymns.

Simple and direct enough to achieve widespread popularity as a children's hymn and a beautiful expression of the author's personal sense of gratitude. The verses of *For the Beauty of the Earth* are also an ideal expression of common experience, highly suitable to the type of corporate worship favored by the

Tracterian reformers as well as for the most personal and informal worship today.

The original refrain, "Christ our God, to thee we raise this our sacrifice of praise," written to be sung as a post-communion prayer in the Anglican service, was later changed to "Lord of all, to thee we raise this our hymn of grateful praise" to make the hymn more suitable for general use as a hymn of praise and thanksgiving. Of the original nine stanzas, no more than five or six are generally included in most modern hymnals. This hymn is usually paired with the tune, "Dix," from a German chorale by Conrad Kocher, arranged by William H. Monk.

Key Lyrics

For the beauty of the earth,
for the beauty of the skies,
for the love which from our birth
over and around us lies,
Refrain:
Christ our God, to thee we raise
this our sacrifice of praise.

Devotional – Grateful Praise

Now, consider these verses from Psalm 107: "O give thanks to the Lord, for he is good; for his steadfast love endures forever. Let the redeemed of the Lord say so...Let them thank the Lord for his steadfast love, for his wonderful works to humankind. And let them offer thanksgiving sacrifices and tell of his deeds with songs of joy. - Psalm 107:1-2a; 21-22

Allow Folliott Sandford Pierpoint's verses to lead your devotional.

For each perfect gift of thine
To our race so freely given, (Name some of these gifts to you.)
Graces human and divine,
Flowers of earth and buds of heaven (Think of your favorite flowers. What are buds of heaven?)

For thyself, best gift divine! (What does this mean to you?)
To our race so freely given; (What race is the author talking about?)

For that great, great love of thine, (In Jesus' sacrificial life!)
Peace on earth and joy in heaven. (What does this mean?)

Prayer
Lord of All,

To You, I raise my personal hymn of grateful praise for all the perfect gifts you have so freely given. And especially for the greatest gift of all – Jesus, our savior!

Amen

Resources **-** http://faithmusicconnection.com/story16

Story # 17
Jesus Christ is Risen Today

Story of the Hymn
Ever hear of something called a "pastiche"???

A pastiche is a literary work or musical composition made up of selections from different works. It is used to help people more easily appreciate a new work by including material already familiar to them.

"Jesus Christ is Risen Today" is a great hymn pastiche. It first appeared, paired with the tune, "Easter Hymn," in 1708. Today, worshipers in both Catholic and protestant churches continue to sing this hymn, particularly on Easter Sunday. Surprisingly, the original author and composer are both unknown.

The first three stanzas of our hymn are from an anonymous, 14th-century Latin, Easter carol – "Surrexit Christus Hodie." "Risen, is Christ today" is a literal translation of the original Latin. John Walsh first published this hymn along with translations of other Latin and German hymns in a 1708 collection.

41 years later, John Arnold published this hymn in "The Compleat Psalmodist," 2nd edition, 1749. This publication included a slightly modified translation of the first stanza, together with completely new second and third stanzas. We sing these stanzas today. Many modern hymnals also include a fourth stanza written by Charles Wesley as a doxology to this great resurrection hymn. Wesley's stanza first appeared in "Wesleyan Hymns and Sacred Poems," published in 1740.

Charles Wesley also wrote an original hymn of 11 stanzas entitled "Christ the Lord is Risen Today. Editors often pair Wesley's hymn with the tune "Easter Hymn." It first appeared in the 1739 London publication, "Hymns and Sacred Poems." "Jesus Christ is Risen Today" is often confused with Wesley's hymn. Both hymns are in the same meter. And we sing both to the same tune with added "Alleluias" at the end of each line of verse. Wesley used the three original stanzas of "Jesus Christ is Risen Today" as stanzas eight, through ten of his hymn. The previously mentioned fourth stanza doxology written by Wesley also adds to the confusion.

Despite any confusion, there is no doubt that Christians everywhere associate "Jesus Christ is Risen Today" with Easter Sunday.

Key Lyrics

Jesus Christ is risen today, Alleluia!
Our triumphant holy day, Alleluia!
Who did once, upon the cross, Alleluia!
Suffer to redeem our loss, Alleluia!

Hymns of praise then let us sing, Alleluia!
Unto Christ, our heavenly King, Alleluia!
Who endured the cross and grave, Alleluia!
Sinners to redeem and save, Alleluia!

Devotional – First Importance

For I handed on to you as of first importance what I in turn had received: that Christ died for our sins in accordance with the scriptures, and that he was buried, and that he was raised on the third day in accordance with the scriptures.– 1 Corinthians 15:3-4

The title of our hymn, "Jesus Christ is Risen Today," is the central theme of Easter in all Christian churches. But is it not also appropriate for every day of the year? Catholic, Orthodox and Protestant churches following a liturgical form of worship based on the Mass and including communion underscore this principle. Because "Jesus Christ is Risen Today," every day is every Christian's "triumphant holy day." Further, Jesus Christ "did once, upon the cross, suffer to redeem our loss." "The pains which He endured, our salvation have procured."

Therefore, All Christians, regardless of denomination, can join in singing "hymns of praise...unto Christ, our heavenly King. Alleluia!" "Now above the sky he's king." Our savior and lord, Jesus Christ, fully human, yet fully divine and one with God, eternally reigns above.

Now, some questions for reflection. How does "Jesus Christ is Risen Today" involve your past? Is "Jesus Christ is Risen Today" a meaningful part of your life today? What does "Jesus Christ is Risen Today" mean to your future? How do your answers involve others?!

Prayer
Almighty God,

Thank you that I can sing of the unspeakable gift— "Jesus Christ is Risen Today."

Alleluia and Amen!

Resources - http://faithmusicconnection.com/story17

Story # 18

Praise to the Lord the Almighty

Story of the Hymn

The modern German city of Düsseldorf gets its name from a nearby small stream, the Düssel brook. Just a few feet wide, its entire length was only 50 miles from its source to where it once flowed into the great Rhein River. Until the middle of the 19th century, this stream meandered through a deep, 60-foot gorge marked by numerous waterfalls, cliffs, caves, and rugged landscape.

After studying theology at the University of Bremen from 1666-1670, Joachim Neander continued his studies at Heidelberg and Frankfort. He moved to Düsseldorf in 1674 and accepted a position at the Lateinschule (grammar school), where he served as both principal and teacher until 1679. Neander greatly enjoyed roaming the rugged terrain of the deep gorge through which the Düssel brook flowed. He is reputed to have read his poems and sung his musical compositions during pilgrimages to the numerous caves and grottos. In addition to his personal pilgrimages, he also taught and preached to groups he guided on spiritual retreats. His well-known love of the area led to its becoming known as the Neanderthal, the German term for Neander Valley.

In 1856, the bones of the "Neanderthal Man" were discovered in this valley, memorializing the surname of this great hymn writer and composer.

This awesome hymn, based on Psalms 150 and 103, verses 1-6, is probably the most popular and widely sung of the many hymns written by Neander. He wrote it in the last year of his life, at the age of 30, shortly before he died of tuberculosis. Catherine Winkworth, 19th-century English scholar, translated the hymn into English and included it in her collection, "Chorale Book for England," published in 1863.

Key Lyrics

Praise to the Lord, the Almighty, the King of creation!
O my soul, praise Him, for He is thy health and salvation!
All ye who hear, now to His temple draw near;
Praise Him in glad adoration.

Praise to the Lord, O let all that is in me adore Him!
All that hath life and breath, come now with praises before Him.
Let the Amen sound from His people again,
Gladly for aye we adore Him.

Devotional – Your Neanderthal

Praise the Lord! Praise God in his sanctuary; praise him in his mighty firmament! Praise him for his mighty deeds; praise him according to his surpassing greatness! Praise him with trumpet sound; praise him with lute and harp! Praise him with tambourine and dance; praise him with strings and pipe! Praise him with clanging cymbals; praise him with loud clashing cymbals! Let everything that breathes praise the Lord! Praise the Lord! –Psalm 150

Bless the Lord, o my soul, and all that is within me, bless his holy name. Bless the Lord, O my soul, and do not forget his benefits – who forgives all your iniquity, who heals all your diseases, who redeems your life from the Pit, who crowns you with steadfast love and mercy, who satisfies you with good as long as you live so that youth is renewed like the eagle's. The Lord works vindication and justice for all who are oppressed. –Psalm 103:1-6

Psalm 150 is like a call to worship for us to praise God with music. And not just vocal music! The psalmist urges us to praise God with instruments—brass, strings, woodwinds and percussion. And, with dance! Joachim Neander and numerous hymn writers through the ages have given us hymns of praise and devotion to answer the psalmist's call to "praise God in his sanctuary."

The psalmist continues, "praise him in his mighty firmament!" And "Let everything that breathes praise the Lord!" Neander gets it. "All that hath life and breath, come now with praises before Him" … "the King of creation."

Where is your "Neanderthal?" Do you worship God there? Who joins you in worship in that place?

Prayer
Creator God,

Let all that is in me adore you! Thank you for being my health and salvation. Give me listening ears to hear the music of all creation and to join in singing your praise.

In Jesus' Name,
Amen

Resources **-** http://faithmusicconnection.com/story18

Story # 19
A Mighty Fortress is Our God

Story of the Hymn

Martin Luther, author and composer of *A Mighty Fortress is our God,* was born in Eisleben, Saxony, in 1483. In 1505, he abandoned law studies to become an Augustinian monk. Two years later he was ordained a priest and preacher in the Saxon city of Wittenberg. Shortly thereafter, he began to study and teach theology at the University of Wittenberg, where he was awarded a doctorate in 1512.

Luther's monumental literary accomplishment was his translation of the Bible into German. He encouraged congregational singing and participation in worship, not just in the church, but also in homes and schools. The following excerpt gives insight into the importance Luther placed on hymns:

That it is good, and pleasing to God, for us to sing spiritual songs is, I think, a truth whereof no Christian can be ignorant; since not only the example of the prophets and kings of the Old Testament (who praised God with singing and music, poetry and all kind of stringed instruments) but also the like practice of all Christendom from the beginning, especially in respect to psalms, is well known to everyone:

yea, St. Paul doth also appoint the same (I Cor. xiv.) and command the Colossians, in the third chapter, to sing spiritual songs and psalms from the heart unto the Lord, that thereby the word of God and Christian doctrine be in every way furthered and practiced.

Accordingly, to make a good beginning and to encourage

others who can do it better, I have myself, with some others, put together a few hymns, in order to bring into full play the blessed Gospel, which by God's grace hath again risen: that we may boast...that Christ is become our praise and our song.

Luther wrote 37 hymns and paraphrases. "A Mighty Fortress is Our God" was published in 1529 in Klug's "Gesangbuch" (songbook). 19th-century American German scholar, Frederick H. Hedge, translated it into English. The English version was published in 1853, in "Hymns for the Church of Christ," edited by Hedge and F. D. Huntington.

Key Lyrics

A mighty fortress is our God, a bulwark never failing;
Our helper He, amid the flood of mortal ills prevailing:
For still our ancient foe doth seek to work us woe;
His craft and power are great, and, armed with cruel hate,
On earth is not his equal.

That word above all earthly powers, no thanks to them, abideth;
The Spirit and the gifts are ours through Him Who with us sideth:
Let goods and kindred go, this mortal life also;
The body they may kill: God's truth abideth still,
His kingdom is forever.

Devotional – Ultimate Refuge

God is our refuge and strength, a very present help in trouble.
Therefore, we will not fear, though the earth should change,
Though the mountains shake in the heart of the sea;
Though its waters roar and foam, though the mountains tremble with its tumult.

"Be still and know that I am God! I am exalted among the nations, I am exalted in the earth." The Lord of hosts is with us; the God of Jacob is our refuge. –Psalm 46:1-3, 10-11

Despite the technological advances of life in the 21st century, the ravages of war, terrorism and despotism remain real. Instead of dialogue and understanding, violence and discord threaten to undermine civility and order in the United States. Along with these threats, hurricanes, earthquakes, volcanoes and floods seem to strike with increasingly deadly frequency.

With so many uncertainties and challenges, how can we find a safe refuge anywhere? Do you feel safe from natural disasters, accidents, serious disease or death? And terrible things seem to continue to happen to good people. Why not you?

Psalm 46, which inspired Martin Luther's "A Mighty Fortress is Our God," does not promise us immunity from the perils of life. But Psalm and hymn remind us that God is our ultimate refuge, with us, even in the worst disasters imaginable.

Prayer
O God, Our Mighty Fortress,

Free me from worry and fear. Give me the faith to trust in you as my refuge and strength. Still my restless spirit and help me to remember and know that you are God.

Amen

Resources **–** http://faithmusicconnection.com/story19

Story # 20
Come Thou Fount of Every Blessing

Story of the Hymn

Robert Robinson was born in 1735 in Swaffham, Norfolk, England, to parents of humble means. He attended Latin school when he was eight. His father died two years later, and his mother reluctantly apprenticed Robert, at the age of 14, to a London barber and hairdresser. However, nearing completion of the apprenticeship, his master, noticing his preference for books over barber duties, released him from his indenture.

On a Sunday afternoon in 1752, Robinson and some friends plied an old fortune-telling woman with drink, so they could make fun of her predictions. With fixed gaze she told Robinson that, unlike his friends, he would live to see his children and grandchildren. Startled, he was struck with the purpose-less life he was leading. That night, he decided to go to hear the preaching of the great evangelist George Whitefield. Much moved by Whitefield's sermon, he spent the next three years in reading and study, during which time his faith developed and deepened. Subsequently, he worked as an assistant to John Wesley and other evangelical preachers.

In 1758, at age 23, Robinson was called as pastor for the Methodist chapel at Mildenhall, Norfolk. There, he wrote "Come Thou Fount of Every Blessing" as a hymn-poem to conclude a sermon he prepared for Whitsunday (Pentecost).

Writing a hymn to conclude sermons was a common practice of 18th-century clergy in England. The best of these hymns were often published—usually without tunes—in various collections that were quite popular among English Christians. They were typically sung to popular Psalm tunes of the late 17th and early 18th-centuries.

Such was the case with our hymn, which was first published in 1759, in "A Collection of Hymns Used by the Church of Christ in Angel Alley, Bishopsgate." In the second stanza, the words, "Here I raise my Ebenezer," refer to a passage from the Old Testament book of First Samuel, which cites "Ebenezer" as the Hebrew word meaning "stone of help." Our hymn first appeared in the United States in a collection published in Germantown, Pennsylvania, in 1791.

Key Lyrics
Come, Thou fount of every blessing,
Tune my heart to sing Thy grace;
Streams of mercy, never ceasing,
Call for songs of loudest praise.
Teach me some melodious sonnet,
Sung by flaming tongues above.
Praise the mount! I'm fixed upon it,
Mount of Thy redeeming love.

Devotional – Due for a Tuning
Then Samuel took a stone and set it up between Mizpah and Jeshanah, and named it Ebenezer; for he said, "Thus far the Lord has helped us." –1 Samuel 7:12

When the day of Pentecost had come, they were all together in one place. And suddenly from heaven there came a sound like the rush of a violent wind, and it filled the entire house where they were sitting. Divided tongues, as of fire, appeared among them, and a tongue rested on each of them. All of them were filled with the Holy Spirt and began to speak in other languages, as the spirit gave them ability. – Acts 2:1-4

In "Come Thou Fount of Every Blessing," Robert Robinson demonstrates knowledge of scripture with his skillful poetic reference to "Ebenezer." The first stanza contains some beautiful musical metaphors of spiritual experience: "Tune my heart to sing thy grace." The finest concert grand piano in the hands of an expert tuner may be prepared for exquisitely beautiful sounds when played by a great artist. Conversely, the same instrument, when out of tune or tuned improperly, can sound "like the devil." Continuing with the first stanza, "Streams of mercy, never ceasing, call for songs of loudest praise. Teach me some melodious sonnet, sung by flaming tongues above." What a powerful statement of the coming of the Holy Spirit at Pentecost!

What about your heart and your life? Are you tuned to be a blessing to God and others? Even the finest pianos need periodic tuning. What about you? Are you due for a tuning?

Prayer
God of Every Blessing,

I confess my life is sometimes so out of tune that I sound like the devil. Please send your Holy Spirit to tune my heart to sing your grace.

In Jesus' Name,
Amen

Resources **-** http://faithmusicconnection.com/story20

Story # 21
Dear Lord and Father of Mankind

Story of the Hymn

John Greenleaf Whittier was born in 1807 on a farm near Hemphill, Massachusetts. His Quaker parents placed a high value on education, but maintaining the family farm was of prime importance. His formal education consisted of two years of study at the nearby Hemphill School, where a teacher introduced him to the works of Robert Burns. This fueled Whittier's life-long interest in poetry and provided a foundation for his development as a writer and poet.

Whittier abhorred slavery, and his deeply held Quaker principles led him to oppose war. But, ultimately, he decided to refocus his work away from politics and toward writing and editing. In 1857, he began an affiliation with the periodical, The Atlantic Monthly, which lasted for the rest of his life.

Throughout his life, Whittier remained in touch with his rural roots, maintaining an empathy with the common man. His poetry enjoyed great popularity both in the United States and in Great Britain. Perhaps his most popular poem is "Snowbound," published in 1866, detailing winter life and landscape near his New England home.

"Dear Lord and Father of Mankind" first appeared in "The Atlantic Monthly," in 1872. It was part of an extended narrative poem entitled, "The Brewing of Soma." The subject was futile attempts of an order of pagan priests to achieve a religious experience by drinking an intoxicating brew. W. Garrett Horder adapted the hymn for congregational singing, including it in a collection entitled, "Worship Song," published in London, in 1884.

Key Lyrics

Dear Lord and Father of mankind,
Forgive our foolish ways;
Reclothe us in our rightful mind,
In purer lives Thy service find,
In deeper reverence, praise.

Breathe through the heats of our desire
Thy coolness and Thy balm;
Let sense be dumb, let flesh retire;
Speak through the earthquake, wind, and fire,
O still, small voice of calm!

Devotional – Still, Small Voice

So then, a sabbath rest still remains for the people of God; for those who enter God's rest also cease from their labors as God did from his.

Since, then, we have a great high priest who has passed through the heavens, Jesus, the Son of God, let us hold fast to our confession. For we do not have a high priest who is unable to sympathize with our weaknesses, but we have one who in every respect has been tested as we are, yet without sin. Let us therefore approach the throne of grace with boldness, so that we may receive mercy and find grace to help in time of need –Hebrews 4:9-10, 14-16

Though written over 135 years ago, John Greenleaf Whittier's hymn, "Dear Lord and Father of Mankind," seems particularly relevant today. Ours is a frantic, fast-paced world of instant news, communication and entertainment interrupted by violence, famine and natural disasters.

Fires floods, earthquakes, volcanoes, hurricanes, tornadoes and tsunamis claim many lives. Many are brought down by alcohol and drug abuse. Perhaps, we are not unconnected with the pagan subjects of the poem of which our hymn is a part.

Whittier invites us to pray with him. "Dear Lord and Father forgive our foolish ways. Take from our souls the strain and stress and reclothe us in our rightful mind. Speak through the earthquake, wind and fire. Breathe through the heats of our desire, thy coolness and thy balm. Drop thy still dews of quietness till all our strivings cease. Let us hear the gracious calling of the Lord and "rise up and follow thee".

Prayer
Dear Lord and Father,

Forgive my foolish ways. Reclothe me in a rightful mind. Allow me to hear your gracious calling and enable me to follow you.

In Jesus' Name,
Amen

Resources - http://faithmusicconnection.com/story21

Story # 22
Our God Our Help in Ages Past

Story of the Hymn

Isaac Watts, author of "Our God Our Help in Ages Past," is universally known as the "Father of English Hymnody." He was born in Southampton, England, in 1674, to devout Calvinistic parents, who were often persecuted for their "non-conformist" beliefs. At a very early age he showed an interest in books and by age thirteen had learned Latin, Greek, French and Hebrew.

At the turn of the 18th century, hymn singing by English-speaking Christians was in a dismal state. For example, Congregational singing was limited to translations of the Old Testament Book of Psalms. Though the Psalms are indeed the "hymnbook" of the Bible, English translations of the day were often hard to sing.

In the preface of his 1719 work about Psalm singing in worship, Isaac Watts writes as follows.

"An Enquiry into the Right Way of Fitting the Book of Psalms for Christian Worship. (Though) The Psalms of David are a work of admirable and divine composure. (though) They contain the noblest sentiments of piety and breathe a most exalted spirit of devotion. Yet, when the best of Christians attempts to sing many of them in our common translations, that spirit of devotion vanishes and is lost. The Psalm dies upon their lips, and they feel scarce anything of the holy pleasure. If this attempt of mine...introduce(s) warm devotion in this part of divine worship, I shall esteem it an honorable service done to the Church of Christ."

"Our God Our Help in Ages Past" first appeared in 1719 in a collection restating the Psalms in New Testament, Christian language. The first two words sometimes appear as "O God" as used in a later hymn collection by John Wesley. However, Watts' original "Our God" is in keeping with English biblical translations of Psalm 90, on which our hymn is based.

Key Lyrics
Our God, our help in ages past,
Our hope for years to come,
Our shelter from the stormy blast,
And our eternal home.

A thousand ages in Thy sight
Are like an evening gone;
Short as the watch that ends the night
Before the rising sun.

Devotional – Through the Ages
Lord, you have been our dwelling place in all generations. Before the mountains were brought forth, or ever you had formed the earth and the world, from everlasting to everlasting you are God. You turn us back to dust, and say, "Turn back, you mortals." For a thousand years in your sight are like yesterday when it is past, or like a watch in the night.
– Psalm 90:1-4

These words are a beautiful statement of faith. Although the original Hebrew text was intended to be sung, this literal English translation is not easy to sing. Now, consider Isaac Watts' version of the same text in "the language of the New Testament suitable for Christian worship."

"Our God, our help in ages past,
Our hope for years to come,
A shelter from the stormy blast
And our eternal home.

Before the hills in order stood,
Or earth received her frame,
From everlasting Thou art God,
To endless years, the same."

Thus, Watts gives us not only another beautiful statement of faith, but also, the wonderful bonus of lyrics we can sing in the spirit of the original verses in ancient Hebrew.

What do Watts' verses mean to you? Why do you think believers still sing "Our God Our Help in Ages Past" 300 years after this hymn was written? Do you recall your parents or grandparents telling you about their faith in God helping them through a difficult situation? When has God helped you get through tough times?

Prayer
Everlasting God,

Forgive me for taking you for granted. Help my unbelief and connect me with my relatives and others who have put their faith in you through the ages. Give me the confidence to live knowing you are ultimately in control.

In Jesus' Name,
Amen

Resources - http://faithmusicconnection.com/story22

Story # 23
America the Beautiful

Story of the Hymn

Katharine Lee Bates is undoubtedly most famous for her poem, "America, the Beautiful."

She was born in Falmouth, Massachusetts, in 1859, daughter of a Congregational minister, who died before her second birthday. Her brothers recognized her intelligence and assured she receive a fine literary education. She earned undergraduate and graduate degrees from Wellesley College, where she later became head of the English department. Bates retained this post for many years until retirement shortly before her death in 1929. She devoted her life's work to education and to the ideal of literature in revealing and developing values.

The beautiful scenery of Pike's Peak, Colorado, particularly inspired Katharine Lee Bates during an 1893 summer sabbatical from her teaching duties. She jotted some notes about the beauty of the landscape into a journal. Interestingly, it was not until two years later that she wrote out the verses of her famous poem. In it she wonderfully describes the expansive views of mountain, plain and sky. Bates also expresses appreciation for her country, governed by law and founded on the principles of liberty, freedom and self-sacrifice. And she strongly believed these natural and political resources were dependent on the continual blessing of God.

The "Congregationalist Newspaper" first printed "America, the Beautiful," in 1895. Following several revisions, the "Boston Evening Transcript" first published it nine years later.

Ironically, it was not intended to be sung, though its meter (the pattern of syllables in lines of poetry) is common to many hymns. Though Katharine Lee Bates wrote many other poems and literary works, none approach the popularity of "America, the Beautiful."

Key Lyrics

O beautiful for spacious skies,
For amber waves of grain;
For purple mountain majesties
Above the fruited plain!
America! America!
God shed His grace on thee,
And crown thy good with brotherhood,
From sea to shining sea.

Devotional – Great and Good

For the Lord your God is bringing you into a good land, a land with flowing streams, with flowing springs and underground waters welling up in valleys and hills, a land of wheat and barley, of vines and fig trees and pomegranates, a land of olive trees and honey, a land where you may eat bread without scarcity, where you will lack nothing, a land whose stones are iron and from whose hills you may mine copper.

Then do not exalt yourself, forgetting the Lord your God, who brought you out of the land of Egypt, out of the house of slavery. But remember the Lord your God, for it is he who gives you power to get wealth, so that he may confirm his covenant that he swore to your ancestors, as he is doing today. –Deuteronomy 8:7-9, 14, 18

Happy is the nation whose God is the Lord, the people whom he has chosen as his heritage.
Psalm 33:12

Katharine Lee Bates clearly expresses her belief that the power of the U.S. government and institutions comes to the people from God above. Her hymn is also a beautiful prayer.

She is reported to have told friends that while many countries may have been great, they failed because they were not good. She feared her country would meet the same fate unless citizens are willing to crown greatness with goodness and bounty with brotherhood.

Are you concerned as was Katherine Lee Bates that your country may fail because it is not good? What would it be like to crown greatness with goodness? How can we crown bounty with brotherhood? What can you do, individually and collectively, to realize Katharine Lee Bates' prayer for your country? Can a country be great and/or good and have flaws?

Prayer
Lord God,

Thank you for loving me even with all my flaws. Thank you for the blessings I and my country enjoy. Empower me to receive the wisdom needed to be a good citizen of my country and your eternal kingdom.

In Jesus Name,
Amen

Resources – http://faithmusicconnection.com/story23

Story # 24
Fairest Lord Jesus

Story of the Hymn
According to legend, 12-century German crusaders sang "Schoenster Herr Jesu" ("Fairest Lord Jesus") as they marched to fight Moslems in Palestine. Whether true or not, the actual author of the hymn is unknown. It first appeared in "Muensterisch Gesangbuch" ("Muenster Songbook"), a Catholic hymnal published in 1677, in Muenster, Westphalia, Germany. German Jesuits in Muenster trace a handwritten manuscript of the Hymn to 1662. The Jesuits (or Society of Jesus) is a Catholic order whose members dedicate themselves to scholarship and devotion to Jesus.

Later, "Fairest Lord Jesus" appeared in an 1842 collection, "Schlesiger Volkslieder (Silesian Folksongs). Heinrich August Hoffman von Fallerslebein (1789-1874) published this collection in Leipzig, Germany, in 1842. He stated he had notated both words and music after hearing them sung by devout Protestant Silesian peasants in Glaz.

Richard Storrs Willis (1819-1900) heard "Fairest Lord Jesus" during graduate studies in Germany. An 1841 Yale alumnus, Willis returned to the United States in 1848 to become music critic for the New York Herald Tribune. Two years later, he published three stanzas, beginning with "Fairest Lord Jesus," paired with the tune "Crusaders' Hymn." This publication, "Church Chorales and Choir Studies," popularized the hymn in the United States.

In 1873, Lutheran minister Joseph Augustus Seiss translated the hymn for use in Sunday School by evangelical Lutherans.

Seiss's translation included two additional stanzas, both beginning "Beautiful Savior." Lutherans today still favor this translation.

Key Lyrics

Fairest Lord Jesus, ruler of all nature,
O Thou of God and man the Son,
Thee will I cherish, Thee will I honor,
Thou, my soul's glory, joy and crown.

Beautiful Savior, Lord of the nations,
Son of God and Son of Man!
Glory and honor, praise, adoration
Now and forevermore be Thine!

Devotional – Above Every Name

Let the same mind be in you that was in Christ Jesus, who though he was in the form of God, did not regard equality with God as something to be exploited. But he emptied himself, taking the form of a slave, being born in human likeness. And being found in human form, he humbled himself and became obedient to the point of death—even death on a cross. Therefore, God also highly exalted him and gave him the name that is above every name. So that at the name of Jesus, every knee should bend in heaven and on earth and under the earth. And every tongue should confess that Jesus Christ is Lord, to the glory of God the Father.
– Philippians 2:5-11.

Hymn writers often write hymns as a direct response to scripture. Consider the first phrase of our hymn— "Fairest Lord Jesus" and Philippians 2:9. *Therefore God also highly exalted him and gave him the name that is above every name.*

Has not the hymn writer given us a beautiful poetic re-statement of scripture? And one we can sing!

Meditate on each line of our hymn. Connect each with phrases from the above scripture from Philippians. Can you also connect phrases of the hymn with other scripture passages? Consider the first chapter of the Gospel of John and the passages from Luke's and Matthew's gospels on the birth of Jesus and his crucifixion and resurrection.

Before ending your meditation, consider what "Fairest Lord Jesus" means to you. What does the life of Jesus suggest about the way you should live your life?

Prayer
Almighty God,

Thank you for loving me even with all my flaws. Thank you especially for Jesus, my beautiful savior. Help me to live in a way that honors you.

In Jesus' Name,
Amen

Resources - http://faithmusicconnection.com/story24

Story # 25
I Love Thy Kingdom Lord

Story of the Hymn
The eighteenth century was a time of evangelism and spiritual revival in both England and America. In the American colonies, the powerful preaching of Jonathan Edwards spearheaded a movement known as the "Great Awakening." Despite this great spiritual revival, congregational singing was mostly confined to metrical versions of the Psalms. This had been the preferred practice since shortly after the landing of the Puritan pilgrims in Plymouth, Massachusetts. Indeed, the 1640 collection known as the "Bay Psalm Book" was the first book of any kind published in the American colonies. Curiously, not until the 1698 ninth edition was music—just thirteen tunes—included with the texts.

The "Great Awakening" led to the publication of many new Psalm settings, including versions by Isaac Watts (1674-1748). Watts wrote metrical versions of the Psalms and hymns based on emotion and experience common to most Christians. He is regarded as the "Father of English Hymnody." Evangelical leaders in England and America highly favored Watts' work.

In 1729, Benjamin Franklin reprinted many of Watts' hymns and Psalm settings in Philadelphia., However, American Christians soon wanted Psalm settings in which King David's words sounded less like those of an Englishman. As a result, American publishers produced many collections of Watts' works revised by American authors.

After the Revolutionary War, controversy arose over which edition of the Psalms should be sung in American Christian denominations. The conflict usually centered on whether to use original settings by Watts and his predecessors or newer American versions.

"I Love Thy Kingdom, Lord" was one of 33 original psalm paraphrases by Dr. Timothy Dwight, grandson of Jonathan Edwards. Dwight included it in his collection under the formal title, "The Psalms of David by Isaac Watts, Revised, 1800." This collection was popularly known as "Dwight's Watts." It included original settings by Dwight as well as revisions of Isaac Watts' Psalm settings. Significantly, Dwight's settings were in language better suited to Christians in the new republic known as the United States of America.

"I Love Thy Kingdom, Lord" is a part of Dwight's metrical setting of Psalm 137. Since the first publication in 1800, Americans continue to sing this hymn. Therefore, it is likely the oldest hymn by an American author still in common use today. Ironically, it is most often paired with the tune, "St. Thomas," by English composer Aaron Williams.

Key Lyrics
I love Thy kingdom, Lord,
The house of Thine abode,
The church our blessed Redeemer saved
With His own precious blood.

Sure as Thy truth shall last,
To Zion shall be given
The brightest glories earth can yield
And brighter bliss of Heaven.

Devotional – Remember and Sing

How could we sing the Lord's song in a foreign land? If I forget you, O Jerusalem, let my right hand wither! Let my tongue cleave to the roof of my mouth, if I do not remember you, if I do not set Jerusalem above my highest joy. –Psalm 137:4-6

The imagery of Psalm 137 evokes emotion that lends itself to full expression in the abstract medium of music. In Giuseppe Verdi's opera, "Nabucco," a chorus of Hebrew slaves recalls memories of happy times at the temple in Jerusalem. Verdi sets all of Psalm 137 in one of the greatest of all opera choruses, "Va Pensiero." The metaphor of the longing of the Italian people for a united Italy was unmistakable.

For Christians today, Psalm 137 is a poignant reminder of the joy of salvation of all believers through Jesus Christ. It may be easy to sing praises to God inside a church surrounded by believers of like spirit. But, outside those friendly walls, the captivity of a less spiritual world lurks. Even St. Peter, the "rock" on whom the church was built, denied, three times, that he knew Jesus.

Have you, like St. Peter, loudly denied that you know Jesus? Or, have you failed to remember Jesus and your call to discipleship? Like Verdi for the Italians, Timothy Dwight, in his paraphrase set to "St. Thomas," allows us to remember and sing.

Prayer
Great God and King,

Forgive me for living without remembering your love for me and your church of all believers. Increase my receptiveness of your divine love and make my life a joyful song of praise to you.

In the Name of Jesus,
Amen

Resources **-** http://faithmusicconnection.com/story25

Story # 26
Come Thou Almighty King

Story of the Hymn
On a calm Sunday morning early in 1783, a congregation of Christians gathered, as usual, for Sunday worship. Their church was on Long Island, New York, not far from New York City. Like all Americans throughout the thirteen colonies, these worshippers were aware of sporadic armed conflicts throughout the land. The occasional skirmishes off the coast between American privateers and British ships were closer to their homes. But for the most part, the war left their everyday lives relatively unchanged.

A small group of British soldiers burst into the church during the service, rudely shattering any complacency these patriotic Christian worshippers may have felt. Their captain stormed to the front of the church and demanded that the entire congregation stand and sing, "God Save the King." After the organist played an introduction, the congregation spontaneously and heartily sang a different hymn to the familiar tune - "Come, Thou Almighty King."

Some authorities attribute authorship to Charles Wesley because it was first published with one of his hymns. However, this seems unlikely. First, Wesley never claimed authorship. Second, it is not included in any of the older hymnals used by English Methodists. Third, the hymn is in a meter not used in any of the other hymns by Wesley.

Andrew Law first published this hymn in America, in Cheshire, Connecticut, 1783, in his "Collection of Hymns for Social Worship." Law was the grandson of a colonial governor of Connecticut and was a prominent composer and music teacher. Although he included hymns from British and American sources, he did not list an author for "Come, Thou Almighty King." The hymn remains anonymous today, though it continues to be quite popular.

Key Lyrics

Come, Thou almighty King,
Help us Thy Name to sing, help us to praise!
Father all glorious, o'er all victorious,
Come and reign over us, Ancient of Days!

Come, holy Comforter,
Thy sacred witness bear in this glad hour.
Thou Who almighty art, now rule in every heart,
And ne'er from us depart, Spirit of power!

Devotional – Spirit of Power

Here is my servant, whom I uphold, my chosen, in whom my soul delights; I have put my spirit upon him; he will bring forth justice to the nations. –Isaiah 42:1
He said to me… "Not by might, nor by power, but by my spirit, says the Lord of hosts." –Zechariah 4:6

For you did not receive a spirit of slavery to fall back into fear, but you have received a spirit of adoption. It is that very spirit bearing witness with our spirit that we are children of God. –Romans 8:15, 16

Jesus said Loving God fully, and your neighbor as yourself are the two greatest commandments. He also said to give to the emperor the things that are the emperor's and to God the things that are God's.

How well are you living up to these teachings? Do you love God above everything else? How about loving your neighbor as yourself? What in your life belongs to "the emperor;" what belongs to God? Who is your "emperor?"

The anonymous 18th-century author of our hymn reminds us we need God's help to follow Jesus' teachings. "Come, Thou Almighty King, help us..." "reign over us." "Come, Holy Comforter...rule in every heart." Every phrase in this hymn is a prayer. Does the hymn sound like any of your prayers?

Prayer
Almighty God,

Forgive me for living first for me. Even my prayers are too often me centered. Please forgive me. May your kingdom come. Rule in my heart and help me to sing your praise.

In Jesus name,
Amen

Resources - http://faithmusicconnection.com/story26

Story # 27
Rejoice the Lord is King

Story of the Hymn

Charles Wesley (1707-1788), author of "Rejoice the Lord is King," is one of the greatest and most prolific hymn writers of all time. He wrote over 6,000 hymns, many of which are still popular today. In these hymns, Charles Wesley expresses a wide range of biblical knowledge and Christian experience in poetic language almost everyone can easily understand.

For over 50 years, Charles Wesley served alongside his brother John, tirelessly preaching and writing hymns with astounding ease and facility. His work greatly advanced the movement for "the people known as Methodists." Interestingly, he maintained his ordination vows as a member of the clergy of the Church of England throughout his life. And he strongly opposed the establishment of a new, separate Methodist denomination.

"Rejoice, the Lord is King!" first appeared in "Moral and Sacred Poems," published by John Wesley, in 1744. Charles Wesley published it again, slightly revised, in his "Hymns for Our Lord's Resurrection," in 1746. Each of the six original stanzas contains a short refrain encouraging the believer to lift both heart and voice. Thus, he combines informed Christian thought and deep emotion in the poetic phrases of this hymn.

Key Lyrics

Rejoice, the Lord is king! Your Lord and king adore;
Mortals give thanks and sing, and triumph evermore;

Lift up your heart, lift up your voice;
Rejoice, again I say, rejoice!

His kingdom cannot fail, He rules o'er earth and Heav'n,
The keys of death and hell are to our Jesus giv'n;
Lift up your heart, lift up your voice;
Rejoice, again I say, rejoice!

Rejoice in glorious hope! Jesus the Judge shall come,
And take His servants up to their eternal home.
We soon shall hear th'archangel's voice;
The trump of God shall sound, rejoice!

Devotional – King of Kings

The Lord is King! Let the earth rejoice! – Psalm 97:1

Rejoice in the Lord always; again, I will say, rejoice!
– Philippians 4:4

He is the reflection of God's glory and the exact imprint of God's very being, and he sustains all things by his powerful word. When he had made purification for sins, he sat down at the right hand of the majesty on high. – Hebrews 1:3

And from Jesus Christ, the faithful witness, the firstborn of the dead, and the ruler of the kings of the earth. To him who loves us and freed us from our sins by his blood, and made us to be a kingdom, priests serving his God and Father, to him be glory and dominion forever and ever. Amen. – Revelation 1:5-6

Charles Wesley skillfully weaves the above scriptures into "Rejoice, the Lord is King!" His inspired poetic gift immediately brings the message of Christ to all—believer, seeker or skeptic. Each stanza includes a refrain based on Philippians 4:4— "Rejoice in the Lord always; again, I will say, rejoice!"

For your own meditation, consider the first phrase of each stanza.
"Rejoice, the Lord is King;" –Is the Lord your king? What kind of subject to the king are you?
"Jesus the Savior reigns;" –Over what? And why?
"His Kingdom cannot fail;" –What kingdom? What does this mean to me?
"He sits at God's right hand;" –What place could be more powerful?
"He all his foes shall quell;" and –Who are these foes?
"Rejoice in glorious hope." –Do you share this glorious hope?

Charles Wesley's wonderful statement of faith and your own response allows you to join countless believers through the ages in singing. "Lift up your heart, lift up your voice; rejoice, again I say, rejoice!

Prayer
Glorious God,

I rejoice that you are king over all and for your great love for me. Lord, show me how to lift up my voice to you each day anew. May your will be done.

In Jesus' Name,
Amen

Resources **-** http://faithmusicconnection.com/story27

Story # 28
From Greenland's Icy Mountains

Story of the Hymn

Reginald Heber was born in 1783, in Cheshire, England, to a wealthy and influential family. A precocious reader from an early age, he received academic honors from his studies in Latin and English literature at Brasenose College, Oxford. He was then ordained in the Church of England and later awarded an honorary doctorate from Oxford University.

After 16 years as vicar at Hodnet in Shropshire, where he wrote most of his nearly 60 hymns, he was appointed Bishop of Calcutta, in 1823. In this new position he was responsible for preaching the Gospel, baptizing new converts and establishing churches throughout the entire Indian sub-continent. This missionary work took a toll on his health, and he died of a stroke in 1826.

Heber displayed a keen interest in missionary work even before his Calcutta appointment. In 1819, he penned his great missionary hymn, "From Greenland's Icy Mountains." "From Greenland's icy mountains to India's coral strand…the heathen in his blindness bows down to wood and stone…Salvation! O Salvation!

The joyful sound proclaim till earth's remotest nation has learned Messiah's name." Amazingly, Heber completed all four stanzas in about a half-hour.

Key Lyrics

From Greenland's icy mountains, from India's coral strand;
Where Afric's sunny fountains roll down their golden sand:
From many an ancient river, from many a palmy plain,
They call us to deliver their land from error's chain!

Waft, waft, ye winds, His story, and you, ye waters, roll
Till, like a sea of glory, it spreads from pole to pole;
Till o'er our ransomed nature the Lamb for sinners slain,
Redeemer, king, creator, in bliss returns to reign!

Devotional – Missionary! Who Me?

Go therefore and make disciples of all nations, baptizing them in the name of the Father and of the Son and of the Holy Spirit, teaching them to obey everything that I have commanded you. And remember, I am with you always, to the end of the age. –Matthew 28:19-20

This great commission, the concluding verses of the gospel of St. Matthew, has inspired Christian missionaries throughout the age. Reginald Heber, like they, committed to share the good news of Jesus Christ to the far reaches of the world.

Perhaps, Heber's hymn led to his missionary appointment as Bishop of Calcutta in 1823. Surprisingly, there seems little in his previous pastoral and scholarly career that suggests success in missionary work. His health was fragile, seemingly unsuited to the rigorous physical demands of serving in the harsh climate of southern Asia. . . except for his ardent devotion to and love for Jesus Christ. Christian missionaries continue to answer the great commission.

The missionary field of India was surely out of Reginald Heber's personal comfort zone. But he answered the call to that place without wavering. Modern idols may be even more powerful than those made of wood and stone. And "heathen" may be a politically incorrect term, today. Do you know non-believers and perhaps even those who mock Christianity? Does the great commission in Matthew's gospel apply to them? To you? To whom do you have a responsibility to share the good news of Jesus Christ?

Prayer
O God,

Your great commission troubles me. I confess to failing to share your gospel even with those in my immediate circle of friends and acquaintances. Sometimes, I live like a heathen. Forgive me. Lead me and show me how to be a missionary for you.

In Jesus' Name,
Amen

Resources - http://faithmusicconnection.com/story28

Story # 29
It Is Well with My Soul

Story of the Hymn

The early 1870s were difficult for Horatio G. Spafford, successful Chicago lawyer and businessman. First, his only son died in 1870. Then he suffered significant real estate losses in the great Chicago fire of 1871. Refusing to despair, he threw himself with renewed vigor into his legal and business affairs.

His efforts were successful and in November 1873, he planned a family vacation to Scotland. Unexpected business demands interrupted these plans. Instead of cancelling, Spafford accompanied his wife and four daughters to New York. There, he booked them on the French steamer "Ville du Havre," planning to meet them a short time later. He then returned to Chicago to complete his pending business transactions.

On November 22, 1873, an English ship collided with the "Ville du Havre." The French ship sank 15,000 feet into the cold Atlantic Ocean within twelve minutes. A few days later, Spafford received a telegram sent by his wife from Cardiff, Wales: "Saved Alone. What shall I do?"

He immediately returned to New York and set sail to join his distraught wife. Reports vary as to when Spafford wrote his only hymn which has provided comfort to so many.

However, all confirm "It is Well with my Soul" was his amazing, inspiring response to the loss of his daughters.

Key Lyrics

When peace, like a river, attendeth my way,
When sorrows like sea billows roll;
Whatever my lot, Thou has taught me to say,
It is well, it is well, with my soul.

Refrain: It is well, with my soul,
It is well, with my soul,
It is well, it is well, with my soul.

And Lord, haste the day when my faith shall be sight,
The clouds be rolled back as a scroll;
The trump shall resound, and the Lord shall descend,
Even so—it is well with my soul.

Refrain: It is well, with my soul,
It is well, with my soul,
It is well, it is well, with my soul.

Devotional – It Is Well

He carried him and brought him to his mother; the child sat on her lap until noon, and he died. "Is the child alright?" She answered, "It will be all right." – 2 Kings 4:20, 26b

Blessed are those who mourn, for they will be comforted. – Matthew 5:4

Beloved, I pray that all may go well with you and that you may be in good health, just as it is well with your soul.
– 3 John 2

Hymns are remarkable, poetic statements of faith of Christians throughout history. They demonstrate an ongoing connection to the earliest believers, whose stories as disciples of Jesus are recorded in the New Testament.

Tragic events often inspire great statements of faith. Few of us will have to endure a string of tragedies such as those faced by Horatio G. Spafford. Somehow, he was able to proclaim, like the Shunammite woman in 2 Kings 4:26, after the death of her only son, "It is well." Though her son was ultimately brought back to life by the prophet Elisha, her faith may have resonated with Spafford. For he already knew, firsthand, after the death of his only son, that tragic circumstances do not always have happy endings.

Some accounts claim Horatio Spafford wrote his hymn as his ship passed over the place in the Atlantic where his daughters had perished just a few days earlier. Other, more reliable accounts claim Spafford wrote it three years later, just before publication.

Which account do you believe? Does it matter when Spafford wrote the hymn? Does when he wrote it affect its meaning and impact? Could sharing the message of "It is well" with someone who has just suffered a devastating loss be hurtful instead of helpful?

Spafford's great hymn continues to comfort and inspire. And it perhaps helps us to empathize with him and with people we know who experience overwhelming pain and sorrow.

Prayer
Lord Almighty,

Thank you for the stories of those who utter "it is well" in the face of devastating pain and loss. Open my eyes to recognize and comfort people around me who suffer. Help me to empathize and show me how to comfort them. Please increase my faith so that "whatever my lot" I, too, can proclaim, "It is Well with my Soul."

In Jesus' Name,
Amen

Resources **-** http://faithmusicconnection.com/story29

Story # 30
I Need Thee Every Hour

Story of the Hymn

Annie Sherwood was born in 1836 in Hoosick, New York, in a beautiful and historic area located thirty-three miles northeast of Albany, just five miles from the border of Vermont. A precocious girl, Annie Sherwood wrote poetry from her early childhood, and by the age of fourteen, her poems were being published in area newspapers. Her family attended Hoosick Baptist Church, and after moving to Brooklyn, New York, where she spent most of her adult life, she married Charles H. Hawks, who became a principal in Knowlson & Company, a prominent Wall Street banking and brokerage firm.

As was the custom of the day, she took the name of her husband, and the couple joined the Hanson Place Baptist Church in Brooklyn. One day as she was doing some housework, she was suddenly stuck by a powerful inspiration of what she later described as a compelling need to fully rely on God in every aspect of her life. She immediately stopped what she was doing and wrote out four beautiful verses now known everywhere as our hymn, *I Need Thee Every Hour.*

She showed the verses to her pastor, Dr. Robert Lowry, himself an accomplished hymn writer and musician. Lowry added a refrain and quickly wrote out the music which he named, *Need,* after the principal theme of the poem.

The hymn was first published in Cincinnati in 1872 in a small collection of hymns intended for use in Sunday schools.

Two years later, this popular new hymn was sung in England, by baritone singing-evangelist Ira D. Sankey, during evangelistic meetings conducted by Dwight L. Moody.

Even with the widespread popularity of *I Need thee Every Hour*, Annie Sherwood Hawkes continued to focus her life on being a devoted wife and mother of three. It was only after the death of her husband at the age of 54, in 1888, after thirty years of marriage, that she began to comprehend the comforting power of the verses she had written: "I did not understand at first why this hymn had touched the great throbbing heart of humanity. It was not until long after, when the shadow fell over my way, the shadow of a great loss, that I understood something of the comforting power in the words which I had been permitted to give out to others in my hour of sweet serenity and peace."

Key Lyrics

I need Thee every hour, most gracious Lord;
No tender voice like Thine can peace afford.

Refrain: I need Thee, O I need Thee;
Every hour I need Thee;
O bless me now, my Savior,
I come to Thee.

Devotional – Always on Call

In the day of my trouble I call on you, for you will answer me. – Psalm 86:7

Let us therefore approach the throne of grace with boldness, so that we may receive mercy and find grace to help in time of need. – Hebrews 4:16

Christians have always looked to the Bible for comfort in times of trouble. Annie Sherwood Hawks knew the above verses. She was not in distress or bereavement but was taking care of housework in her home when she was struck by an overwhelming sense of a need for total reliance on Jesus in every aspect of her life. Such were the rather ordinary circumstances leading to the inspiration resulting in our hymn. It was years later, at the death of her husband of thirty years, that she understood the comforting power of her inspired hymn. The words of Jesus in John 15:5 continue to call us as they undoubtedly touched and inspired Annie Sherwood Hawks: "I am the vine; you are the branches. Those who abide in me and I in them bear much fruit, because apart from me you can do nothing." We like she, "need thee every hour."

Prayer

Gracious Lord,

I am so grateful that I can call on you in times of trouble and difficulty. Help me to rely on you for all my needs. Sharpen my awareness of opportunities to serve you and others in the ordinary moments of my life.

In Jesus' Name,
Amen

Resources **-** http://faithmusicconnection.com/story30

Story # 31
Praise my Soul the King of Heaven

Story of the Hymn
Queen Elizabeth II honored Henry Francis Lyte when she included the singing of this hymn in her royal wedding on November 20, 1947, exactly 100 years after his death.

Henry Francis Lyte was born in Scotland in 1793 and spent most of his childhood in an orphanage. He had a keen intellect, attending Trinity College in Dublin, Ireland, with the intent of becoming a physician; however, his scholarly interest in theology and English Poetry together with his strong personal faith led to his ordination as an Anglican minister in 1815. He was appointed pastor of All Saints Church of Lower Brixham, Devonshire, in 1824, serving there for thirty years until weeks before his death from tuberculosis in 1847.

The scholarly, poetic Henry Lyte, of fragile health and bothered by asthma, was a kind and compassionate man, an excellent and beloved pastor who gave himself wholeheartedly in service to the simple folk of the small fishing community. He found time to write two books of religious poetry and dozens of hymns, the two most famous being *Praise My Soul, the King of Heaven*, based on Psalm 103, and *Abide With Me*, which he completed just three weeks before his death.

Key Lyrics
Praise, my soul, the King of Heaven;
To His feet thy tribute bring.
Ransomed, healed, restored, forgiven,

Evermore His praises sing:
Alleluia! Alleluia!
Praise the everlasting King.

Father like He tends and spares us;
Well our feeble frame He knows.
In His hands He gently bears us,
Rescues us from all our foes.
Alleluia! Alleluia!
Widely yet His mercy flows.

Devotional – Fit for a Queen

Praise the Lord! Praise the Lord from the heavens; praise him in the heights! Praise him, all his angels; praise him, all his host! Praise him, sun and moon; praise him, all you shining stars! Praise him, you highest heavens, and you waters above the heavens! Let them praise the name of the Lord, for he commanded, and they were created.

Kings of the earth and all peoples, princes and all rulers of the earth! Young men and women alike, old and young together! Let them praise the name of the Lord, for his name alone is exalted; his glory is above earth and heaven. – Psalm 148:1-5, 11-12

Let the word of Christ dwell in you richly; teach and admonish one another in all wisdom; and with gratitude in your hearts sing psalms, hymns, and spiritual songs to God.
– Colossians 3:16

Christians have always sung praises to God. The "king of heaven" has that title because God is the creator of all and thus, worthy of praise. Singing is uniquely personal: intimate when voiced by a solo singer and uplifting when shared by a large group of worshippers. Isn't our faith like that – intimate yet uplifting when shared?

"Praise him for his grace and favor" to believers who have lived before us and to us because God is "slow to chide" (scold) "and swift to bless."

"Fatherlike he tends and spares us," God gently holds us in his hands in this life and the next.

"Frail as summer's flower we flourish," but God is unchanging in his wisdom, power and love.

"Angels, help us to adore him" along with sun, moon and everything that exists in time and space.

"Alleluia! Alleluia! Praise with us the God of grace."

Prayer
O King of Heaven,

Open my heart to the harmony of your awesome power and your perfect love. Empower my voice to sing your praises and enable me to be slow to scold and swift to bless.

In Jesus' Glorious Name,
Amen

Resources **-** http://faithmusicconnection.com/story31

Story # 32
All the Way my Savior Leads Me

Story of the Hymn

The late 19th and early 20th centuries were times of great spiritual revival and evangelistic fervor in the United States. Fanny Crosby's spirit and talent were ideally suited for the times. Her hymns of simple and direct expression of personal Christian experience were in great demand by composers and publishers.

Published with tunes of simple melodies and harmonic structure, these easily learned and remembered hymns became known as "Gospel Songs."

Biglow and Main published most of her hymns. This company was a combination of the publishers of two principle compilers of gospel songs, Philip P. Bliss and Ira D. Sankey. Among her many hymns still popular today are "Blessed Assurance," "Jesus is Tenderly Calling Thee Home," "Tell Me the Story of Jesus," "I am Thine, O lord, I Have Heard Thy Voice," "Jesus, Keep Me Near the Cross," "Pass Me Not, O Gentle Savior," "Rescue the Perishing" and "To God be the Glory, Great Things he Hath Done."

"All the Way, my Savior Leads Me," came to Fanny Crosby at home as she meditated on the goodness of God. A friend wrote out the verses for her and sent them to Robert Lowry. He quickly composed the music known as "All the Way."

Robert Lowry and William H. Doane first published hymn and tune in 1875, in the Sunday School collection, "Brightest and Best."

Key Lyrics

All the way my Savior leads me;
What have I to ask beside?
Can I doubt His tender mercy,
Who through life has been my guide?
Heav'nly peace, divinest comfort,
Here by faith in Him to dwell!
For I know, whate'er befall me,
Jesus doeth all things well;
For I know, whate'er befall me,
Jesus doeth all things well.

Devotional – Ask for Directions

You show me the path of life. In your presence there is fullness of joy; in your right hand are pleasures forevermore. – Psalm 16:11

Then Moses lifted up his hand and struck the rock twice with his staff; water came out abundantly, and the congregation and their livestock drank. – Numbers 20:11

The Lord alone guided him; no foreign god was with him. – Deuteronomy 32:12

For surely I know the plans I have for you, says the Lord, plans for your welfare and not for harm, to give you a future with hope. – Jeremiah 29:11

Consider "I am Thine, O Lord," by Fanny Crosby. She wrote this hymn in 1875, the year "All the Way, my Savior Leads Me" was published. Perhaps, this hymn can be your prayer in difficult times as well as when you lack inspiration. May it lead you to proclaim with Fanny Crosby, "All the Way, my Savior Leads Me."

I am Thine, o Lord, I have heard Thy voice,
And it told Thy love to me;
But I long to rise in the arms of faith,
And be closer drawn to Thee.

Refrain
Draw me nearer, nearer, blessed Lord,
To the cross where Thou hast died;
Draw me nearer, nearer, blessed Lord,
To Thy precious, bleeding side.

O the pure delight of a single hour
That before Thy throne I spend,
When I kneel in prayer, and with Thee, my God,
I commune as friend with friend!

Refrain

Consecrate (dedicate) me now to Thy service, Lord,
By the power of grace divine;
Let my soul look up with a steadfast hope,
And my will be lost in Thine.

Refrain

Prayer
Divine Comforter,

You alone, know the best path for my life. Thank you for showing me the way to live. Forgive me for failing to ask you for directions and for stubbornly trying to go my own way. Give me the wisdom and heavenly peace to follow your leading and when I am lost, to seek your will.

In Jesus' Name,
Amen

Resources - http://faithmusicconnection.com/story32

Story # 33
Joyful, Joyful, We Adore Thee

Story of the Hymn
Ever hear of Beethoven?

The place is Vienna, Austria. The time is the evening of May 7, 1824. A large audience has gathered for the premier performance of a new symphony. Though eccentric and temperamental, the local composer had become a favorite of Viennese concertgoers.

An hour passes. The customary four movements of the standard symphony, interrupted only by short pauses between, are complete. But there is no applause. This new work is already over twice as long as earlier symphonies by this composer. Even so, the audience expectantly and eagerly listens as a fifth movement begins. First, an introduction restates important musical themes from each of the previous four movements.

Next, the orchestra sounds a new melody. Surprisingly, a baritone soloist then forcefully sings the first lines of Friedrich Schiller's "Ode to Joy." Soprano, alto and tenor soloists, together with a large chorus of singers, bring this massive work to a stirring conclusion.

The audience, overwhelmed, momentarily sits in stunned silence. Then, they jump to their feet in thunderous applause and shouts of appreciation of this musical masterpiece of classical symmetry and romantic yearning.

Hunched over the score with his back to the audience, the composer, totally deaf for several years, continues to conduct. He is oblivious of the stupendous ovation until gently turned around by the alto soloist. This unleashes a flood of renewed cheering and applause, continuing long into the evening.

Such was the setting for the first public performance of Beethoven's Ninth Symphony. The principal melody of the final movement provides the tune for a most powerful hymn of praise – "Joyful, Joyful, We Adore Thee."

Presbyterian pastor and Princeton Professor of English Henry van Dyke wrote the "Joyful, Joyful, We Adore Thee" lyrics in 1907. At the time, he was serving as guest preacher at Williams College in the Berkshire Mountains of Western Massachusetts. Inspired by the beautiful scenery of the Berkshires, he presented the hymn to Williams College president, Harry A. Garfield. Van Dyke also specified that it be sung to the music of Ludwig van Beethoven's, "Hymn to Joy." Editors of the Presbyterian Hymnal included it in a new 1911 edition.

Key Lyrics

Joyful, joyful, we adore Thee,
God of glory, Lord of love;

All Thy works with joy surround Thee,
Earth and heaven reflect Thy rays,

Thou our Father, Christ our brother,
All who live in love are Thine:
Teach us how to love each other,
Lift us to the joy divine.

Devotional – Surrounded by Joy
When the morning stars sang together, and all the heavenly beings shouted for joy. – Job 38:7

Be glad in the Lord and rejoice, O righteous, and shout for joy, all you upright in heart. – Psalm 32:11

Rejoice always, pray without ceasing, give thanks in all circumstances; for this is the will of God in Christ Jesus for you. – 1 Thessalonians 5:16-18
Non-German-speaking people rarely have an opportunity to consider the beautiful poetry of Friedrich Schiller's "Ode to Joy." I invite you to consider and ponder this translation of the complete German text.

O Friends, no more these sounds! Let us sing more cheerful songs, more full of Joy! Joy, bright spark of divinity, daughter of Elysium (In Greek mythology, a place or state of perfect happiness), fire-inspired we tread thy sanctuary. Thy magic power re-unites all that custom has divided. All men become brothers under the sway of thy gentle wings. Whoever has created an abiding friendship, or has won a true and loving wife, all who can call at least one soul theirs, join in our song of praise...Even the worm can feel contentment, and the cherub stands before God!

Gladly, like the heavenly bodies which He set on their courses through the splendor of the firmament, brothers you should run your race. As a hero going to conquest, you millions, I embrace you. This kiss is for all the world! Brothers, above the starry canopy there must dwell a loving Father. Do you fall in worship, you millions? World, do you know your Creator? Seek Him in the heavens! Above the stars must he dwell.

Prayer
God of Glory, Lord of Love,

Thank you for surrounding me with the joy of living in the beauty of your creation. Thank you for being like a loving parent and for the gift of Christ as my eternal brother and friend. Enable me to love you better. Teach us all to love each other and lift us to your joy divine! Amen.

Resources **-** http://faithmusicconnection.com/story33

Story # 34
For All the Saints

Story of the Hymn
William Walsham How (1823-1897, author of "For All the Saints," was known as the "Poor Man's Bishop" for his genuine care for the poor in East London during the 1880s. In addition to his pastoral duties in the Church of England, he wrote over fifty hymns. "For All the Saints" first appeared in an 1864 collection entitled, "Hymns for Saints' Days."

This hymn is a meditation and commentary on the phrase, "I believe in the communion of the saints," from the Apostles' Creed. It is also based, in part, on Hebrews, chapter 12. Of How's eleven original stanzas, most modern hymnals include only six or fewer.

Other hymns by How include, "O Jesus, Thou art Standing," "We Give Thee but Thine Own" and "O Word of God Incarnate."

Ralph Vaughan Williams (1872-1958) composed the tune, "Sine Nomine," (Latin for "without name") specifically for "For All the Saints." As editor, he included hymn and tune in "The English Hymnal," published in 1906.

Vaughan Williams composed important symphonies, operas, ballets, chamber music, music for films, and art songs in addition to much sacred music. His music often reflects a deep mysticism and sincere Christian faith. He contributed several original tunes and almost 40 folk tune arrangements in addition to his work as editor of "The English Hymnal."

Also, he edited "The Oxford Book of Carols," published in1926, the definitive collection of English carols. Today, he is universally recognized as one of the most important composers of the 20th century.

Key Lyrics

For all the saints, who from their labors rest,
Who Thee by faith before the world confessed,
Thy name, O Jesus, be forever blessed.
Alleluia, Alleluia!

From earth's wide bounds, from ocean's farthest coast,
Through gates of pearl streams in the countless host,
And singing to Father, Son and Holy Ghost:
Alleluia, Alleluia!

Devotional – In the Cloud

Therefore, since we are surrounded by so great a cloud of witnesses, let us also lay aside every weight and the sin that clings so closely, and let us run with perseverance the race that is set before us, looking to Jesus, the pioneer and perfecter of our faith, who for the sake of the joy that was set before him endured the cross, disregarding its shame, and has taken his seat at the right hand of the throne of God.

Pursue peace with everyone and the holiness without which no one will see the Lord.

Therefore, since we are receiving a kingdom that cannot be shaken, let us give thanks, by which we offer to God an acceptable worship with reverence and awe. – Hebrews 12: 1-2, 14, 28

"Saints' Day Hymn—Cloud of Witnesses"—was the original title of "For All the Saints." Consider the connection of our hymn with the passages from Hebrews 12. Can you sense a connection modern Christians have with the lives of faith lived out by generations of Christians of earlier times?

"For All the Saints" and indeed every Christian hymn, ancient and modern, are a mystical and compelling expression of this connection. The Apostles Creed states this as "the communion of the saints." Think of "saint" as one who believes and lives out their Christian calling. Do you have a relative who helped you grow in faith? Are you inspired by a saint that lived in a different time? Is it harder to be a saint and a witness now than it was in earlier times? Why? Why not? Do you consider that your life as a believer could be an inspiration to others?

Prayer
God of Past, Present and Future,

Thank you for the "cloud of witnesses" who have known you and have inspired and helped me in my walk of faith. Increase my awareness of their impact on my life and help me to follow their examples in living out the faith. Empower me to be a saint to the people in my life – family, friends, acquaintances and those I do not even know.

In the Name of Jesus,
Amen

Resources - http://faithmusicconnection.com/story34

Story # 35
Joy to the World

Story of the Hymn

"Joy to the World," one of the most joyous and popular hymns associated with Christmas, was not originally intended as a Christmas carol. Instead, author Isaac Watts (1674-1748) wrote it as a paraphrase (a rewriting of verses so that they can be easily sung) of Psalm 98:4-9, focusing more on the second coming of Christ.

In this paraphrase Watts, with poetic grace, beautifully restates the Psalm text into lyric Christian verse. He includes both Old and New Testament theology of Christ as child and king, ironically creating a wonderful hymn for both Advent and Christmas. "Joy to the World" first appeared in 1719 in a collection restating the Psalms in New Testament, Christian language.

American composer, church musician and music educator Lowell Mason (1792-1872) wrote the music—entitled "Antioch," for "Joy to the World." He published this in Boston, in 1839, in his collection, "Modern Psalmist."

Mason attributed the basis for "Antioch" to the music of George Frideric Handel (1685-1757). Ironically, Handel and Watts were contemporaries in London. But there is no conclusive evidence of any origin other than of Mason himself. He added a two-line refrain to Watts' original four lines of verse per stanza by repeating the last lines. This addition adds musical emphasis to these important phrases of text.

Key Lyrics

Joy to the world, the Lord is come!
Let earth receive her King;
Let every heart prepare Him room,
And Heaven and nature sing.

He rules the world with truth and grace,
And makes the nations prove
The glories of His righteousness,
And wonders of His love.

Devotional – Make Some Noise

Make a joyful noise to the Lord, all the earth; break forth into joyous song and sing praises. Sing praises to the Lord with the lyre and the sound of melody. With trumpets and the sound of the horn make a joyful noise before the King, the Lord.

Let the sea roar, and all that fills it; the world and those who live in it. Let the floods clap their hands; let the hills sing together for joy at the presence of the Lord, for he is coming to judge the earth. He will judge the world with righteousness, and the peoples with equity. – Psalm 98:4-9

And from the throne came a voice saying, "Praise our God, all you his servants, and all who fear him, small and great." Then I heard what seemed to be the voice of a great multitude, like the sound of many waters and like the sound of mighty thunderpeals, crying out, "Hallelujah! For the Lord our God the Almighty reigns." – Revelation 19:5-6

"Joy to the World" is a beautiful paraphrase of Psalm 98. It encompasses Old and New Testament passages on the coming of Christ and his ultimate kingship over heaven and earth.

Watts phrases the entire hymn in present tense. This connects the past—the birth of Jesus—the present and the future—the apocalyptic return of Christ. Because of this synthesis, we can appropriately sing this hymn at any time of the year.

According to Psalm 98, "all the ends of the earth make a joyful noise to the Lord." Watts poetically synthesizes these phrases into, "Let every heart prepare him room, and heaven and nature sing!" Two centuries later, Mason provided melody for these lyrics which continues to resonate in our hearts.

Questions to ponder. How do you prepare room in your heart for the Christ child at Christmas? Are you prepared for the second coming of Jesus? Do you discount it because you think it won't happen in your lifetime? How is preparing your heart for Christmas like preparing your heart for Jesus' return? How is it different?

Prayer
Righteous Ruler of Heaven and Earth,

Thank you for your awesome power and perfect love. Help me to prepare room in my heart to receive your love and to share it with others. Enable me to make some noise by living in a way that is harmonious with the joyful song of heaven and nature until you come again to rule with truth and grace.

In Jesus' Name,
Amen

Resources - http://faithmusicconnection.com/story35

Story # 36
O Come, O Come, Emmanuel

Story of the Hymn
"O Come, O Come Emmanuel" is a compilation of Latin antiphons—verses spoken or sung around passages of scripture. By the twelfth century, antiphons became standardized as a response to the song of Mary—the "Magnificat" from Luke's gospel.

These antiphons were first arranged into a hymn published in the German city of Cologne in 1710. Subsequently, this hymn was translated into English by John Mason Neale in 1851. Ten years later it was altered for inclusion in the London, first edition of "Hymns Ancient and Modern."

"O Come, O Come Emmanuel" has now achieved world-wide popularity. Most significantly, it has brought increased awareness of the season of Advent as a preparation for Christmas.

Neale (1818-1866) translated almost 400 hymns and authored the children's Christmas carol, "Good King Wenceslas." Son of a Church of England clergyman, he earned baccalaureate and master's degrees from Cambridge. There, he developed interests in the study of ancient hymns and architecture.

After ordination, his health prevented him from carrying out full-time pastoral duties. But he was influential in initiating architectural reforms leading to renovation of many English churches.

He also helped establish the St. Margaret's Society, the first Anglican order of nuns dedicated to serving the poor.

Key Lyrics

O come, o come, Emmanuel,
And ransom captive Israel,
That mourns in lonely exile here
Until the Son of God appear.
Refrain: Rejoice! Rejoice!
Emmanuel shall come to thee, o Israel.

O come, desire of nations, bind
In one the hearts of all mankind;
Bid thou our sad divisions cease,
And be Thyself our king of peace.
Refrain: Rejoice! Rejoice!
Emmanuel shall come to thee, o Israel

Devotional – God is With You

"Look, the virgin shall conceive and bear a son, and they shall name him Emmanuel," which means, "God is with us." – Matthew 1:23

"The kingdom of this world has become the kingdom of our Lord and of his Messiah, and he will reign forever and ever." – Revelation 11:15b

"O Come, O Come, Emmanuel" is a beautiful canticle (a hymn or chant with a biblical text, forming part of a church service) derived from passages of scripture on the coming of Christ. "Emmanuel" is a Hebrew word meaning "God is with us." Christians traditionally use the weeks encompassing the four Sundays before Christmas as a time of meditation on the incarnation of "Emmanuel" in the baby Jesus.

Many non-Christians join Christians during this time in the exchange of gifts, parties and expressions of good will. But Christians can also joyfully proclaim the song of Mary, Mother of Jesus, from the first chapter of the Gospel of Luke. "My soul magnifies the Lord, and my spirit rejoices in God my Savior…For the mighty one has done great things for me, and holy is his name. His mercy is for those who fear him from generation to generation."

Prayer
Great Emmanuel,

Thank you for loving us so much that you became a human being, knowing joy and sorrow, desire and pain, yet without sin. You said, whoever sees you, sees God. For you were and are Emmanuel – "God is with us." Thank you for paying the penalty for my sin through your horrible death on the cross. And for the most wonderful gift of eternal life through your resurrection. Enable me to live and share this great news not only at Christmas, but every day.

Come, Emmanuel!
Amen

Resources **-** http://faithmusicconnection.com/story36

Story # 37
Come, Thou Long-Expected Jesus

Story of the Hymn

"Come, Thou Long-expected Jesus" first appeared in a collection by Charles Wesley, "Hymns for the Nativity of our Lord." Published in London, in 1745, he wrote these hymns for congregational singing and personal reading during the season of Advent. Wesley encouraged personal reflection and renewed conviction of faith in preparation for Christmas. Subsequently, twenty-four editions of this collection were published during his lifetime.

Charles Wesley was born at Epworth, Lincolnshire, England, on December 18, 1707. His mother provided his early education at home, which prepared him to excel at the Westminster School, London.

He continued his studies at Christ Church College, Oxford, continuing as a tutor after graduation. He remained at the university until ordination in the Church of England in 1735.

Charles Wesley preached of a loving God, who laid aside aspects of divinity to take on human form for the ultimate salvation and benefit of all who would believe. He preached out-of-doors and in secular buildings to great numbers of people.

A remarkable preacher, he expressed profound truths of the Christian faith in a manner even the uneducated could easily follow. So compelling and persuasive was his preaching, that he often converted his most determined opponents.

In addition to preaching, Charles Wesley is considered by some scholars to stand among the finest English poets of the 18th century. But he is universally recognized as one of the greatest and most prolific hymn writers of all time.

Wesley wrote over 6500 hymns, many of which are still popular today. He expresses a wide range of Christian experience in subjective poetic language with a decidedly evangelical emphasis. In addition to "Come, Thou Long-expected Jesus," are the following favorites:
"A Charge to Keep I Have;"
"Christ the Lord is Risen Today;"
"Love Divine, All Loves Excelling;"
"Ye Servants of God, Your Master Proclaim;"
"Jesus, Lover of my Soul;" and
"Hark the Herald Angels Sing."

Key Lyrics

Come, thou long-expected Jesus
Born to set thy people free;
From our fears and sins release us,
Let us find our rest in thee.

By thine own eternal spirit
Rule in all our hearts alone;
By thine all-sufficient merit,
Raise us to thy glorious throne.

Devotional – Earth-Shaking Gift

For thus says the Lord of Hosts: Once again, in a little while, I will shake the heavens and the earth and the sea and the dry land; And I will shake all the nations, so that the treasure of all nations shall come, and I will fill this house with splendor, says the Lord of hosts. – Haggai 2:6-7

See that you do not refuse the one who is speaking; for if they did not escape when they refused the one who warned them on earth, how much less will we escape if we reject the one who warns from heaven! At that time his voice shook the earth, but now he has promised, "Yet once more I will shake not only the earth but also heaven." – Hebrews 12:25-26

In Come Thou Long-expected Jesus, Charles Wesley refers to both the incarnation and to the second coming of Jesus. Scripture declares that Jesus will then rule eternally as a king over a new heaven and earth.

During the season of Advent—roughly the time between Thanksgiving and Christmas Day—how much time do you spend attending parties and celebrations?

Sending Christmas cards and greetings?

Selecting gifts for family and friends?

Preparing for family gatherings?

As Christians we have every reason to celebrate.

Now consider how much time you spend preparing your heart to allow Jesus, born a child and yet a king, to reign forever.

Where are your priorities?

Prayer
Eternal God,

Thank you for your earth-shaking gift of Jesus, born to set me free from the power of sin. By your own eternal spirit, come into my heart and rule forever. And empower me to live as your worthy subject.

In the name of Jesus,
Amen

Resources **-** http://faithmusicconnection.com/story37

Story # 38
Hark! the Herald Angels Sing

Story of the Hymn

In the early Christian church, Christmas was celebrated for a much longer period than is the custom today. The celebration continued for at least twelve days, sometimes lasting into the month of February.

Liturgical churches, such as Catholic, Episcopal and Lutheran, continue to formally celebrate Christmas over a period of about two weeks. Several fine hymns belong to this season, focusing on the incarnation of God in the infant Jesus. Charles Wesley, (1707-1788) wrote one of the most joyous and popular of these hymns – "Hark! the Herald Angels Sing." It first appeared in 1739 in "Hymns and Sacred Poems." In 1753, Evangelist George Whitefield published several alterations which continue to be used today.

Felix Mendelssohn, (1809-1847) important composer of the Romantic style period, composed the music now associated with this hymn. He wrote it as a chorus for male voices to commemorate the four-hundredth anniversary of Gutenberg's invention of the printing press with moveable type. William Hayman Cummings (1831-1915), noted British musician, adapted the music for use with "Hark the Herald Angels Sing." He named this tune "Mendelssohn" and published it with the hymn in London, in 1857.

Key Lyrics

Hark! the herald angels sing,
"Glory to the newborn king;
Peace on earth and mercy mild,

God and sinners reconciled!"
Joyful, all ye nations rise,
Join the triumph of the skies;
With the angelic host proclaim,
"Christ is born in Bethlehem!"

Refrain: Hark, the herald angels sing,
"Glory to the newborn King!"

Devotional – Singing with Angels

And suddenly there was with the angel a multitude of the heavenly host, praising God and saying, "Glory to God in the highest heaven, and on earth peace among those whom he favors!" – Luke 2:13-14

And the Word became flesh and lived among us, and we have seen his glory, the glory as of a father's only son, full of grace and truth. – John 1:14

Can you imagine celebrating Christmas without music? Consider the sense of peace felt and shared when we sing, "Silent Night, Holy Night." Or the wonder of, "What Child is This?" The sense of joy and anticipation of "O Come, All Ye Faithful." Beautiful, poetic words for sure, but even with the holy events and response they describe, how much more compelling and meaningful they are when sung.

Music has a power to invite, to connect us with each other and to draw us into the presence of God. Mysteriously, music seems to simultaneously remind us of Christmases past and present and to give us hope for Christmases future. And the sounds of music stay with us.

Charles Wesley compels us to give heed (hark!) to the song of the angels on the night Christ was born in Bethlehem: "Glory to the new-born king; Peace on earth and mercy mild, God and sinners reconciled." Then, he encourages our proper response: "Joyful, all ye nations, rise, join the triumph of the skies, With the angelic host proclaim, 'Christ is born in Bethlehem!'"

Other stanzas include these theologically rich verses: "Veiled in flesh the Godhead see; Hail the incarnate deity." And "Jesus, our Emmanuel" (God is with us) and "Light and life to all He brings, Risen with healing in His wings." Felix Mendelssohn's music allows for a full-throated voicing from singers skilled or novice, adding great dimension to the text.

Prayer
God of Light and Life,

Thank you for opportunities to join with the angelic choir in singing your glory. Tune my heart and my voice so that I may better proclaim your message of peace and reconciliation at Christmas and throughout the year.

In Christ's Name,
Amen

Resources - http://faithmusicconnection.com/story38

Story # 39
We Three Kings

Story of the Hymn

How would one go from law school to writing a classic Christmas song?

John Henry Hopkins, Jr. (1820-1891) was a multi-talented man whose first call was to the Episcopal Church. He served as a parishioner, deacon, seminary professor and music teacher, priest and pastor. In addition, he found time to design church seals and stained-glass windows and to illustrate books. He also delivered a eulogy at the funeral of U.S. President Ulysses S. Grant in 1885.

After graduation from the University of Vermont with baccalaureate and master's degrees in 1845, Hopkins moved to New York City. There, he began a career as a journalist with plans to study law. But, the call of the church was greater.

He entered the General Theological Seminary of New York City, graduating in 1850. Soon, he distinguished himself in the field of church music, becoming editor of "The Church Journal" in 1853. He retained this post for fifteen years. In 1855, the seminary appointed him its first Professor of Church Music.

Hopkins wrote "We Three Kings" for a Christmas festival at the seminary in 1857.

He published it in 1863, in his collection, "Carols, Hymns, and Songs." It is a theologically rich hymn. In its stanzas, each of the three kings offers a gift to the Christ child and explains the symbolism. The final stanza and refrain invite all Christians to reflect and offer praise— "king and God and sacrifice."

Hopkins' music for "We Three Kings" is entitled "Kings of Orient." It is one of the relatively few hymns written in a minor key. This tonality (sound quality of the music) suggests the exotic nature of the three kings themselves. It also invites contemplation of the profound significance of the birth of the Christ child and our response.

Key Lyrics

We three kings of Orient are;
Bearing gifts, we traverse afar,
Field and fountain, moor and mountain,
Following yonder star.

Glorious now behold Him arise;
King and God and sacrifice;
Alleluia, alleluia,
Sounds through the earth and skies.

Refrain: O star of wonder, star of light,
Star with royal beauty bright,
Westward leading, still proceeding,
Guide us to thy perfect light.

Devotional – The Whole Story

In the time of King Herod, after Jesus was born in Bethlehem of Judea, wise men from the East came to Jerusalem, asking, "Where is the child who has been born king of the Jews? For we observed his star at its rising and have come to pay him homage."

When they had heard the king, they set out; and there, ahead of them, went the star that they had seen at its rising, until it stopped over the place where the child was. When they saw that the star had stopped, they were overwhelmed with joy. On entering the house, they saw the child with Mary his mother; and they knelt down and paid him homage. Then, opening their treasure chests, they offered him gifts of gold, frankincense and myrrh. – Matthew 2:1-2, 9-11

The hymn poetically elaborates on the purpose of the journey and the symbolic meaning of the gifts the magi brought. Gold would crown the new-born king, who will ultimately reign forever over all. Frankincense represents incense befitting worship of God in prayer and praise.

Myrrh is for the body of the savior who would grieve, bleed, die and lie in the "stone-cold tomb." The final stanza anticipates Jesus' glorious resurrection. "King and God and Sacrifice" is to be worshipped with "Alleluias" sounding "through the earth and skies."

Thus, the Christmas story is complete. The wondrous birth of the Messiah, Emmanuel—God with us—is more than a message of "Peace on Earth, Goodwill to All." It is also the good news of Christ our Savior.

Christ bears the sins of the whole world through death on the cross and resurrection. Ultimately, Christ reigns over a new heaven and a new earth where all who believe are eternally reconciled with God. Alleluia! Amen!

Prayer
Divine Author of Every Good Story,

Thank you for your perfect gift of Christ our savior. Like the star for the wise men, may your Holy Spirit guide me to your perfect light. Let your light lead me in living out the story that you wrote for me so that my life may be a gift to you and others.

In Jesus' Name,
Amen

Resources - http://faithmusicconnection.com/story39

Story # 40
When Morning Gilds the Skies

Story of the Hymn

"When Morning Gilds the Skies" is an English translation of an 18th-century German hymn whose author is unknown. Ironically, two translations remain in use: one by a clergyman; the other by a poet.

Edward Caswall (1814-1878) translated the hymn into English in 1849. Son of an Anglican priest, Caswall graduated with honors from Brasenose College, Oxford. The Church of England ordained him a priest in 1840. Influenced by the Oxford Movement's emphasis on greater piety and formality of liturgy, he switched to Roman Catholicism in 1847. His wife also converted. After her untimely death, he began his work of translating Latin and German texts into English.

Caswall included "When Morning Gilds the Skies" in his "Lyra Catholica" (Catholic Song Lyrics), published in London, in 1849. He also included "Jesus, the Very Thought of Thee"—perhaps, the most widely sung of his translations—in this collection. Ordained a Catholic priest in 1852, he fulfilled his new calling until his death in 1878.

English poet Seymour Bridges (1844-1930) also translated and paraphrased this German hymn for his Yattendon Hymnal of 1899. Educated at Eton and Corpus Christi College, Oxford, Bridges practiced medicine for several years. Ill health brought about his retirement to full-time writing.

British *Poet Laureate* from 1913 until his death, Bridges wrote many volumes of poetry, articles and plays. He also wrote hymn translations, including *Ah, Holy Jesus, O Gladsome Light* and *Jesu, Joy of Man's Desiring.*

Hymn editors continue to include *When Morning Gilds the Skies* in modern hymnals, often mingling stanzas by both Caswall and Bridges.

Key Lyrics

When morning gilds the skies
My heart awaking cries:
May Jesus Christ be praised!
Alike at work and prayer,
To Jesus I repair:
May Jesus Christ be praised!

Devotional – Heart Awakening

Besides this, you know what time it is, how it is now the moment for you to wake from sleep. For Salvation is nearer to us now than when we became believers – Romans 13:11

How do you begin your day? Do you pray? Do you praise and thank God for another day?

From ancient times, world religions have encouraged devout adherents to meditate or pray before going to sleep at night and upon awakening the next morning. The brain is most responsive at these times to the effects of thoughts and impressions that shape daily activities. Evensong and Morning Prayer are examples of corporate Christian worship at the end and beginning of the day. Christians have observed these liturgies for centuries.

Consider the association of sleep with death and night in this popular children's prayer.

"Now I lay me down to sleep,
I pray the Lord my soul to keep.
If I should die before I wake,
I pray the Lord my soul to take."

And, Christians everywhere continue to celebrate Sunday morning worship since the discovery of Jesus' resurrection on that first Easter morning. Through the particular work of Edward Caswall and Joseph Barnby, we have a most fitting hymn to greet each new day. "*When Morning Gilds the Skies, my heart awaking cries, May Jesus Christ be praised.*"

Prayer
God of Light,

Thank you for the gift of each new day. Forgive me for rushing into my daily activities, forgetting you and taking for granted your many blessings. Awaken my heart, so that I can proclaim, "May Jesus Christ be praised" every day.

Amen

Resources - http://faithmusicconnection.com/story40

Story # 41
Beneath the Cross of Jesus

Story of the Hymn

Elizabeth Cecilia Douglas Clephane, a devout Scottish Presbyterian, is the author of "Beneath the Cross of Jesus." Born in Edinburgh in 1830, she was the youngest of three daughters of Andrew Clephane, sheriff of Fife and Kinross. Elizabeth lived most of her life in nearby Melrose in the Abbottsford area. Sir Walter Scott, also a resident, has beautifully described this place.

Elizabeth Clephane's father died while she was very young. Though of fragile health herself, she took a keen interest in the poor and downtrodden. Accordingly, she and her sisters gave much of their family wealth to alleviate their suffering. Thus, she became known as the "sunbeam" of Melrose for her philanthropic devotion.

Elizabeth Clephane wrote poetry and several hymns, which were published in newspapers and in religious publications. Of her hymns, only two are well-known today— "The Ninety and Nine" and "Beneath the Cross of Jesus." She wrote the latter hymn while bed-ridden, shortly before her death in 1869, at age 38. Both hymns were published in 1872, in the Scottish Presbyterian periodical, "The Family Treasury." Ira Sankey encountered them while serving as evangelist Dwight L. Moody's music associate in Scotland. Later, he popularized these hymns in the United States.

"Beneath the Cross of Jesus" is rich in metaphor and many scriptural allusions. William Arnot, editor of "The family Treasury," described this hymn as follows. "These lines express the experiences hopes and the longings of a young Christian lately released. Written on the very edge of life, with the better land fully in view of faith, they seem to us footsteps printed on the sands of time, where these sands touch the ocean of eternity. These footprints of one whom the Good Shepherd led through the wilderness into rest, may, with God's blessing, contribute to comfort and direct succeeding pilgrims."

Key Lyrics

Beneath the Cross of Jesus, I fain would take my stand,
The shadow of a mighty rock within a weary land;
A home within the wilderness, a rest upon the way,
From the burning of the noon-tide heat, and the burden of the day.

Devotional – On the Edge of Life

May I never boast of anything except the cross of our Lord Jesus Christ, by which the world has been crucified to me, and I to the world. – Galatians 6:14

And I heard a loud voice from the throne saying, "See, the home of God is among mortals. He will dwell with them; they will be his peoples, and God himself will be with them; he will wipe every tear from their eyes. Death will be no more; mourning and crying and pain will be no more, for the first things have passed away." – Revelation 21:3-4

The cross, instrument of suffering, torture, humiliation, and slow, agonizing death is at the center of the Christian faith. It forever reminds the believer of the wonders of God's sacrificial, redeeming love. Jesus' death on a cross is also a permanent reminder of the consequences of our personal sin.

The "empty" cross reminds us of the risen Lord Jesus, who overcame our arch-enemy death. It also stands as a symbol of ultimate hope, both universal and intensely personal. Elizabeth Clephane beautifully expresses this hope in her hymn.

"Beneath the cross of Jesus, I fain would take my stand…I take, o cross, thy shadow for my abiding place…My sinful self, my only shame; my glory all, the cross."

Prayer

Redeeming God,

Thank you for the wonders of your love. Open my eyes and my heart to see my own guilt in Jesus' death on the cross. Enable me to humbly and gratefully accept your redeeming love. Empower me to live in the hope of your promise of a time when my home will be with you and death and pain will be no more.

In Jesus' Name,
Amen

Resources - http://faithmusicconnection.com/story41

Story # 42
Come, We That Love the Lord

Story of the Hymn

During the latter part of the 19th century, United States Christians emphasized educational programs for children. This emphasis led to the creation of many new gospel hymns known as "Sunday School Songs." The ideal gospel hymn included a catchy tune, (usually with a refrain) easily learned and remembered, supported by simple harmonies. One of the best of these is "Come, We that Love the Lord."

Isaac Watts, (1674-1748) known as the "Father of English Hymnody," is the author of "Come, We that Love the Lord." This hymn combines references to Psalm 98 and to scriptures describing worship of God in heaven. Watts wrote over 600 hymns, including many new paraphrases (re-writing lines of verse so that they can be easily sung) of the Psalms.

Isaac Watts served the Mark Lane Independent Chapel, London, as pastor from 1702 until his death in 1748. For the last 36 years of his life he lived at the estate of Sir Thomas Abney in Hertfordshire.

Watts' health was frail and the Abney's looked after him in return for his tutoring their children. He evidently enjoyed working with them. His "Divine and Moral Songs for Children," published in 1715, continues to be popular today.

Robert Lowry (1826-1899) was born in Philadelphia, in 1826. He enjoyed a long and successful career as a pastor, preacher, author, editor, professor of literature, composer and hymn writer.

Lowry adapted "Come, We that Love the Lord" and added a refrain. He also composed a sprightly new tune for the adapted hymn: "Marching to Zion." Bigelow and Main first published this new pairing of hymn and tune in 1868, in a collection entitled, "Silver Spray."

Lowry is one of the relatively few hymn writers who also composed music for hymns. He wrote words and music to his most famous hymn, "Shall We Gather at the River," in 1864.

Key Lyrics
Come, we that love the Lord,
And let our joys be known;
Join in a song with sweet accord,
Join in a song with sweet accord
And thus surround the throne,
And thus surround the throne.

Refrain:

We're marching to Zion,
Beautiful, beautiful Zion;
We're marching upward to Zion,
The beautiful city of God.

Devotional – Marching to Zion
And the ransomed of the Lord shall return and come to Zion with singing; everlasting joy shall be upon their heads; they

shall obtain joy and gladness, and sorrow and sighing shall flee away. – Isaiah 35:10

O sing to the Lord a new song, for he has done marvelous things. His right hand and his holy arm have gotten him victory. The Lord has made known his victory; he has revealed his vindication in the sight of the nations. He has remembered his steadfast love and faithfulness to the house of Israel. All the ends of the earth have seen the victory of our God. Make a joyful noise to the Lord, all the earth; break forth into joyous song and sing praises." – Psalm 98:1-4

The Gospels testify that Jesus sang a hymn with his disciples following their last meal together, shortly before his death and resurrection. Eighteen and nineteen centuries later, Isaac Watts and Robert Lowry share their love of Jesus with us.

Because of their poetic and musical gifts, we can simultaneously meditate, rejoice and sing together. "Come, We that love the Lord…From faith and hope, let our songs abound, and every tear be dry. We're marching through Immanuel's ground, to fairer worlds on high."

Questions to ponder:

Who are we that love the Lord?

How do we let our songs abound?

What is Immanuel's ground? (See Matthew 1:22-23)

What is marching to Zion? Why "marching" instead of "walking" or "flying?"

Prayer
Omnipotent Heavenly Father,

Thank you for the psalms that Jesus and his disciples sang. Thank you, also, for hymns to sing your praises. Guide my steps so that my life may join with all children of God in a great song of praise as we march to Zion, where everlasting joy will be upon us and every tear be dry.

In the Name of Jesus Christ,
Amen

Resources **-** http://faithmusicconnection.com/story42

Story # 43
All People that on Earth do Dwell

Story of the Hymn
Have you ever been somewhere where you felt like you didn't belong?

William Kethe, author of our hymn, is thought to have been born in Scotland around the turn of the 16th century. However, there is almost no documentation of his life until the reign of Mary, "Queen of Scots," from 1551-1558. During this time, he is known to have joined English and Scottish Protestant exiles who settled in Geneva to escape persecution. Kethe remained in Geneva after 1858 to work with a group of English scholars on an English translation of the Bible.

This translation became known as the "Geneva Bible" or "Breeches Bible." The practice of singing metrical Psalm settings in French was well-established in Geneva. Psalm singing also gained a foothold in England following publication of a collection in English by John Hopkins. Sternhold and Hopkins published an Anglo-Genevan Psalter around 1556 for use by English religious exiles in Geneva.

"All People that on Earth Do Dwell" is one of 25 metrical (arranged for singing) Psalm versions authored by William Kethe.

An expanded edition of the Anglo-Genevan Psalter, published in 1561, included these Kethe Psalm settings. Our hymn also appeared that year in London, along with French Psalm tunes popular in Geneva. Many scholars consider it to be the oldest metrical Psalm setting still in common use today.

Louis Bourgeois, born in Paris about 1510, was already a prominent composer when John Calvin persuaded him to come to Geneva. Calvin realized the importance of easily sung tunes to support Psalm singing in worship, and Bourgeois skillfully executed this important work.

Of Bourgeois' many original Psalm tunes, "Old Hundredth," published in the 1551 edition of the Genevan Psalter, is undoubtedly the most famous. Many modern hymnals retain the original rhythm of sustained notes at the beginning and end of each line of text. As mentioned above, editors almost always pair "Old Hundredth" with "All People that on Earth Do Dwell." However, many worshippers around the world also sing "Old Hundredth" with the Doxology, "Praise God, from Whom All Blessings Flow."

Key Lyrics
All people that on earth do dwell,
Sing to the Lord with cheerful voice,
Him serve with fear, His praise forthtell;
Come ye before Him and rejoice.

For why? The Lord our God is good;
His mercy is forever sure.
His truth at all times firmly stood,
And shall from age to age endure.

Devotional – Attitude of Praise
Make a joyful noise to the Lord, all the earth. Worship the Lord with gladness; come into his presence with singing. Know that the Lord is God. It is he that made us, and we are

his; we are his people, and the sheep of his pasture. Enter his gates with thanksgiving, and his courts with praise. Give thanks to him, bless his name. For the Lord is good; his steadfast love endures forever, and his faithfulness to all generations.
– Psalm 100

To whom do you belong? To yourself? Your country? Your spouse or partner? Your family? Your profession? Your club? Your creditor? You could probably make a long list of connections that are important (essential?) in your life.

For the moment, consider just four of your answers to the question of to whom you belong.

How do you feel about each of them?

What is your attitude?

Do you feel grateful?

Do they make you happy?

How much of your time do you devote to them?

Are you angry or resentful?

Would you like to change any of them?

Now, read or re-read Psalm 100 above. "Know that the Lord is God. It is he that made us, and we are his; we are his people and the sheep of his pasture."

The Psalmist and the hymn writer leave no doubt as to whom we belong and why: God, because God made us. We are described as sheep, animals that flourish only under the attentive care of a good shepherd. Much of the psalm describes the attitude we should have – joyful, glad, thankful, reverent, full of praise. It concludes with a statement of faith and hope that is over 2,000 years old: "The Lord is good; his steadfast love endures forever, and his faithfulness to all generations."

Prayer

Faithful Father,

Thank you for your enduring love for me and for psalms and hymns that show me how to respond. Help me to build a discipline so that I may enthusiastically worship you and joyfully live to honor you and serve others.

In Jesus' Name,
Amen

Resources - http://faithmusicconnection.com/story43

Story # 44
Love Divine, All Loves Excelling

Story of the Hymn
Charles Wesley (1707-1788) was a compelling preacher, but he is universally recognized as one of the greatest and most prolific hymn writers of all time. He wrote over 6500 hymns, many of which are still popular today. In addition to "Love Divine, All Loves Excelling" are the following favorites:

"A Charge to Keep I Have;"
"Christ the Lord is Risen Today;"
"Come, Thou Long-expected Jesus;"
"Ye Servants of God, Your Master Proclaim;"
"Jesus, Lover of my Soul;" and
"Hark the Herald Angels Sing."

Charles Wesley first published "Love Divine, All Loves Excelling" in a 1747 collection of hymns for an evangelistic campaign. The title was "Hymns for Those that Seek and Those that Have Redemption in the Blood of Jesus Christ." Wesley often preached on the love of God. "Love Divine, All Loves Excelling" effectively supported this theme. The hymn has remained popular and is sung today with several different tunes in the United States and Great Britain.

Key Lyrics
Love divine, all loves excelling,
Joy of Heav'n to earth come down;
Fix in us thy humble dwelling;
All thy faithful mercies crown!
Jesus, Thou art all compassion,
Pure unbounded love Thou art;

Visit us with Thy salvation;
Enter every trembling heart.

Finish, then, Thy new creation;
Pure and spotless let us be.
Let us see Thy great salvation
Perfectly restored in Thee;
Changed from glory into glory,
Till in Heav'n we take our place,
Till we cast our crowns before Thee,
Lost in wonder, love, and praise.

Devotional – In Wonder, Love and Praise

For I am convinced that neither death, nor life, nor angels, nor rulers, nor things present, nor things to come, nor powers, nor height, nor depth, nor anything else in all creation, will be able to separate us from the love of God in Christ Jesus, our Lord. – Romans 8:38-39

Has a hymn ever grabbed you? Perhaps you hear a hymn that was sung at the death of someone dear to you. Or a hymn may remind you of a particularly happy time in your life. Sometimes the sound and feel of voices and instruments joined in a hymn may bring goosebumps or tears. And just the awareness of people around us joining together in singing hymns in worship can be deeply moving, enhancing solidarity and connection.

What is your favorite hymn? How did you learn it? When did you first hear it? Do you associate it with particular people, places or events in your life? When was the last time you sang it?

Charles Wesley's great hymn invites and challenges us to embrace God's "Love Divine, All Loves Excelling." How?

— by serving, praying and praising without ceasing "'til in heaven we take our place, lost in wonder, love and praise." How incredible it will be to join the heavenly choir! What an awesome sound and scene that must be! Meanwhile, for over 270 years "Love Divine, All Loves Excelling" has resonated in the hearts and voices of Christians everywhere.

Prayer
Loving God,

You are the source of all love. I marvel at the wonder of how Jesus came from Heaven to earth in order to give us eternal salvation. Thank you for loving me. Thank you for the wonderful gift of making me a new creation. I praise how you restore my soul through music and hymns so that I can sing your praises and to connect me with you and others. May my voice and my life be pleasing to you through the grace of our Lord Jesus Christ.

Amen

Resources - http://faithmusicconnection.com/story44

Story # 45
Just as I Am

Story of the Hymn
Have you ever felt worthless?

Charlotte Elliott was born in 1789, in Clapham, England, the daughter of a successful silk merchant. Her family were devout believers, including a grandfather and a brother who were Anglican priests. She received an education that led her to a love of poetry and music. A serious illness at age thirty left her medically disabled for the remainder of her life. Her weakened physical condition caused mental distress and feelings of worthlessness, despite her considerable literary talents.

Before her father's death in 1833, Charlotte Elliott met many important religious leaders who were guests at the family home. Noted Swiss evangelist, H. A. Malan, was one of these visitors. During after- dinner conversation, he asked her if she were a true Christian. She dismissed the question but was troubled by it. Several days later, she told Malan she wanted to come to Christ but didn't know how. The evangelist replied, "Why not come just as you are?" This reply inspired the resolution of her struggle, resulting in the verses for which she is now most remembered. "Just as I am, without one plea…O Lamb of God, I come."

Our hymn was first published in an 1836 collection entitled, "The Invalid's Hymn Book." (note – This title was meant to inspire or encourage those who were disabled. During the 19th century, "invalid" did not have the negative connotation it sometimes has today.)

Later that year, she added a seventh stanza for her collection, "Hours of Sorrow Cheered and Comforted."

"Just as I am" has been translated into numerous languages. Today, it continues to be one of the most popular hymns of personal devotion.

Key Lyrics

Just as I am—without one plea,
But that Thy blood was shed for me,
And that Thou bidst me come to Thee—
O Lamb of God, I come, I come.

Just as I am—though tossed about
With many a conflict, many a doubt,
Fightings and fears within, without—
O Lamb of God, I come, I come.

Devotional – Just as You Are

Jesus said to them, "I am the bread of life. Whoever believes in me will never by thirsty. But I said to you that you have seen me and yet do not believe. Everything that the Father gives me will come to me, and anyone who comes to me I will never drive away. For I have come down from heaven, not to do my own will, but the will of him who sent me…This is indeed the will of my Father, that all who see the Son and believe in him may have eternal life. And I will raise them up on the last day." – John 6:35-40

Two years before her death, Charlotte Elliott wrote, perhaps, her most intimate hymn. The following stanza provides insight into her personal faith and inspiration for us.

"O Jesus, make Thyself to me,
A living bright reality:
More present to faith's vision keen,
Than any outward object seen;
More dear, more intimately rich,
Than e'en the sweetest earthly tie."

May we respond to the call of Jesus as did Miss Elliott and countless saints through the ages. "Just as I Am…O Lamb of God, I come! I come!

Prayer
O Lamb of God,

Thank you for your promise that anyone who comes to you, you will never drive away. I confess that I often struggle with doubts, conflicts and fears. Forgive me for the pride of wanting to do something to earn or be worthy of your gift of eternal life. Enable me to trust fully in you and to come to you, "Just as I am."

In Your Name,
Amen

Resources **-** http://faithmusicconnection.com/story45

Story # 46
O Sacred Head Now Wounded

Story of the Hymn

What do you consider an "old" hymn? Your grandmother might say "Blessed Assurance, Jesus is Mine" is one of the great, old hymns. But Fanny Crosby wrote it in the late 19th century.

"O Sacred Head Now Wounded" is attributed to a 12th-century French cleric and saint, Bernard of Clairvaux (1090-1153). Lutheran cleric Paul Gerhardt (1607-1676) translated Bernard's hymn from Latin to German. American Presbyterian pastor and Princeton Theological Seminary professor of church history James Waddell Alexander (1804-1859) translated it into English.

Alexander's translations of Latin and German hymns appeared in an 1861 posthumous collection entitled "The Breaking Crucible and Other Translations." Since then, "O Sacred Head Now Wounded" has been widely used in English hymnals throughout the world.

For over 350 years editors have paired this hymn with a tune originally composed for an early 17th-century love song. Master composer J. S. Bach (1685-1750) arranged and harmonized this tune, renamed "Passion Chorale." A devout Lutheran, Bach used "Passion Chorale" repeatedly throughout his great oratorio, (a large-scale work with orchestra, chorus and soloists based on a religious subject) the "St. Matthew Passion." The chorale was the basis for the listener's reflection and participation.

Bach used "Passion Chorale" for similar purpose in his "Christmas Oratorio" as well. Thus, he connected it to celebration or preparation for both Christmas and Easter. He also used it for thematic material in several of his sacred cantatas and in an organ prelude. Bach's several four-part harmonizations of this chorale may be found in many hymnals.

Key Lyrics

O sacred Head, now wounded, with grief and shame weighed down,
Now scornfully surrounded with thorns, Thine only crown;
O Sacred Head, what glory, what bliss till now was Thine!
Yet, though despised and gory, I joy to call Thee mine.

What language shall I borrow to thank Thee, dearest friend,
For this Thy dying sorrow, Thy pity without end?
O make me Thine forever, and should I fainting be,
Lord, let me never, never outlive my love to Thee.

Devotional – Pure Justice and Love

For to this you have been called, because Christ also suffered for you, leaving you an example, so that you should follow in his steps. 'He committed no sin, and no deceit was found in his mouth.' When he was abused, he did not return abuse, when he suffered, he did not threaten; but he entrusted himself to the one who judges justly. He himself bore our sins in his body on the cross, so that, free from sins, we might live for righteousness; by his wounds you have been healed. For you were going astray like sheep, but now you have returned to the shepherd and guardian of your souls... – 1 Peter 2:21-25

Christians continue to meditate on the passion, crucifixion, death and resurrection of Jesus Christ. His death was not a gentle, peaceful passing, but a horrible, cruel, lingering and excruciatingly painful one. God incarnate chose to die for the reconciliation of all of us to God.

What an example of love and how to live! Jesus suffered and died for you and me so that free from the penalty of our sin, we might live for righteousness. What does that mean? Consider Jesus' example. When he was abused, he did not return abuse. When he suffered, he did not curse or threaten. He lived a blameless life without sin, trusting in God, the ultimate judge who judges justly. Where else can you find pure justice?

Now, reread the first sentence from the above passage from first Peter.

Prayer

Loving and Just God,

When I consider the awful suffering and death of Jesus Christ on the cross, I am overwhelmed by your great love and your almighty, merciful justice. My own sin added to your grief and pain. Forgive me, Lord. Renew me and shepherd me that I might live for righteousness, doing justice, loving kindness and walking humbly with you.

In Jesus' Holy Name,
Amen

Resources - http://faithmusicconnection.com/story46

Story # 47
Lift High the Cross

Story of the Hymn
Do you know the meaning of the word "crucifer?"

For over 2,000 years the cross has been a powerful symbol in western culture. Many nations feature the cross in their national flag; a red cross signifies medical or humanitarian relief. Examples from literature and the arts include the stories of Count Dracula and Faust, in which the cross is used to repel the evil power of the vampire and Mephistopheles. To Christians, the cross represents the ultimate expression of the love of God in the death and resurrection of Jesus Christ for all humanity, motivating believers to active faith and mission. Among the hymns expressing this power of the cross is a product of the work of two, Church of England clergy and one of the most influential church musicians of the 20th century.

George William Kitchin (1827-1912) served the church in a variety of roles, including tutor of the crown prince of Denmark, select preacher at Oxford and Dean of Winchester Cathedral. He originally wrote "Lift High the Cross" for an 1887 festival service at Winchester Cathedral. The sight of the cross atop a long staff carried by a crucifer (the person who carries the cross in a religious procession) seems to have been the inspiration for this, his only hymn.

Michael Robert Newbolt (1874-1956 was ordained an Anglican priest in 1900. Like Kitchin he is also chiefly remembered for his association with "Lift High the Cross." It is his alteration of this hymn for inclusion in the 1916 edition of the influential British hymnal, "Hymns Ancient and Modern," that has become the most widely used in current hymnals, most of which utilize the refrain and no more than five of the original 11 stanzas.

Unlike the authors of "Lift High the Cross," who are both remembered principally for this hymn, Sydney Hugo Nicholson (1875-1947) achieved distinction as one of the most important English church musicians of the first half of the 20th century. He served as organist at Westminster Abbey. From 1913 until his death Nicholson served as music editor of "Hymns Ancient and Modern." For the 1916 edition, he composed the tune named "Crucifer" specifically for "Lift High the Cross." It was immediately popular and is today included in many hymnals.

Key Lyrics
Refrain:
Lift high the cross,
The love of Christ proclaim
Till all the world adore
His sacred name.

Devotional – Triumphal Procession
But Thanks be to God, who in Christ always leads us in triumphal procession, and through us spreads in every place the fragrance that comes from knowing him.
– 2 Corinthians 2:14

Have you been a part of a procession – a group of individuals moving along in an orderly manner? Perhaps as part of a high-school or college graduation ceremony? A wedding? A political protest march? Or a parade? Do you remember any flags or banners that were part of the procession?

What was your mood?

Were you generally looking down or upward?

"Lift High the Cross" is closely connected to Christian processions where leaders of worship enter the church following a cross held high by a crucifer.

This hymn and the above scripture invite us to look up to the cross, the symbol of Christ's redeeming love. Both hymn and scripture suggest that our individual lives are part of a great procession of believers, throughout history and into the future. And that we proclaim Christ's love "till all the world adore his sacred name."

Will you join this great procession?

Prayer
Triumphant God,

Thank you for your redeeming love through Jesus Christ. Thank you also for your gift of music and hymns to sing your praise. Help me to never lose sight of the cross. Show me how to live so that I may be a part of your triumphal procession proclaiming Christ's love.

In Jesus' Name,
Amen

Resources - http://faithmusicconnection.com/story47

Story # 48
Crown Him with Many Crowns

Story of the Hymn

Ever hear of a story of one hymn and two authors?

The evangelical revival of the 18th century brought about unprecedented changes in the staid Church of England. The influence of John and Charles Wesley led to a rise in congregational singing. They emphasized hymns stressing subjective experience and personal devotion. Though hymn singing flourished, musical and liturgical standards varied greatly. In contrast, a group of reformers known as the Tractarians urged a return to more formal, liturgical worship.

During the 1830s, Tractarian reformers published a series of pamphlets about church history and doctrine. These publications had a powerful impact.

One, was a renewed interest in the ideals of the Catholic Church before the Reformation. Two, was a new emphasis on the liturgical hymn, closely related to the liturgical season and context.

Poet and scholar Matthew Bridges (1800-1894) converted to Catholicism in response to these ideals. In 1851, he wrote "Crown Him with Many Crowns" based on Revelation 19:12— "On his head were many crowns." Each of the six stanzas relates to a different crown— "many crowns," "virgin's Son," "Love," "Peace," "Years," and "heaven."

Godfrey Thring (1823-1903), Anglican priest, wrote a hymn on the same text in 1874, upon request of Anglican clergy who opposed the Tractarians.

Thring describes the crowns as follows: "gold," "Son of life," "Lord of light," "Lord of life," "Lord of lords" and "heaven." Thring's supporters intended to replace Bridges' hymn with the one written by Thring.

Both Bridges' and Thring's hymns beautifully reflect the Revelation text. Bridges' hymn as included in 1868, in "Hymns Ancient and Modern," paired with the tune "Diademata," by George J. Elvey, proved too popular to replace.

Hymn editors generally use Bridges' stanzas, beginning with "Crown Him with Many Crowns," sometimes in combination with a few by Thring. Ironically, the hymn was widely popular among both evangelicals and Tractarians. And it remains a favorite today.

Key Lyrics

Crown Him with many crowns,
The Lamb upon His throne.
Hark! How the heavenly anthem drowns
All music but its own.
Awake, my soul, and sing
Of Him who died for thee,
And hail Him as thy matchless king
Through all eternity.
Crown Him the Lord of peace,
Whose power a scepter sways
From pole to pole, that wars may cease,
And all be prayer and praise.
His reign shall know no end,

And round His pierced feet
Fair flowers of paradise extend
Their fragrance ever sweet.

Devotional – Unconditional Victory

He shall judge between the nations and shall arbitrate for many peoples; they shall beat their swords into plowshares, and their spears into pruning hooks; nation shall not lift up sword against nation, neither shall they learn war anymore. – Isaiah 2:4

His eyes are like a flame of fire, and on his head are many diadems; and he has a name inscribed that no one knows but himself. On his robe and on his thigh he has a name inscribed, "King of Kings and Lord of Lords." – Revelation 19:12, 16

Our hymn is a beautiful meditation on the nature of our resurrected Lord Jesus Christ.

"Crown Him the Lord of love" (What love is greater?)

"Crown Him the Lord of peace" (Will forces of evil give up without a fight for ultimate victory?)

"Crown Him the Lord of years, …of time (God reigns over all creation, including time itself!)
Creator of the rolling spheres, ineffably sublime."

"All hail, Redeemer, hail! For Thou hast died for me; (How can you "hail" Jesus?)
Thy praise and glory shall not fail throughout eternity."

Prayer
All-Powerful God,

The powers of evil, darkness and death seem to be all around me. Thank you for the assurance that you are ultimately in control. Forgive me of my sin and increase my faith and show me how to "hail" Jesus and be an instrument of your peace.

In the Name of Jesus Christ,
Amen

Resources - http://faithmusicconnection.com/story48

Story # 49
O for a Closer Walk with God

Story of the Hymn

Did you know that one of the great hymn writers likely suffered from a mental illness that is quite common today?

At the age of 21, William Cowper (1731-1800) suffered the first of many bouts of depression that crippled his adult life. Always a keen observer of his surroundings and his own feelings, depression often drove him to utter despair. Many of these spells of deep depression came upon him during the month of January.

Such symptoms suggest he also may have suffered from what is today called seasonal affective disorder. This condition is marked by melancholia thought to be brought about by the relatively lesser daylight of winter days.

During these episodes, Cowper (pronounced "KOO-purr") made several unsuccessful attempts to commit suicide. A chance meeting with John Newton, curate of the Anglican congregation at Olney, ultimately led to a deepening of his faith. Cowper expressed this in writing 68 hymns for a most important and influential evangelical hymnal, known as the "Olney Hymns." "O for a Closer Walk with God" is from this collection. Significantly this hymnal helped bring evangelical hymns into services of the Church of England.

Newton, former captain of slave ships, had had a spiritual conversion of his own which led him to renounce slavery. He wrote the great hymn, "Amazing Grace." As outgoing and persuasive as Cowper was sensitive and withdrawn, the two worked together effectively to end slavery in Great Britain. However, neither the meaningful work of writing hymns and poetry nor his deep friendship with Newton could keep his depression from returning.

Cowper's personal faith was Calvinistic—he believed that "once saved, always saved." However, when stricken with severe depression, he wrote that he himself was the one exception to this belief. Ironically, "O for a Closer Walk with God" beautifully expresses the calmness and serenity of the believer who is close to God.

Key Lyrics

O for a closer walk with God,
A calm and heavenly frame,
A light to shine upon the road
That leads me to the Lamb!

Return, O holy Dove, return,
Sweet messenger of rest;
I hate the sins that made Thee mourn
And drove Thee from my breast.

So shall my walk be close with God,
Calm and serene my frame;
So purer light shall mark the road
That leads me to the Lamb.

Devotional – A Permanent Cure

Restore to me the joy of your salvation and sustain in me a willing spirit. – Psalm 51:12

Do you suffer from depression or mental illness? Or do you know someone who does?

Modern treatments of prescription medications sometimes supplemented by psychotherapy were unavailable during William Cowper's lifetime. Then, people with mental illness also suffered from the idea that they were somehow at fault for their illness.

However, many continue to suffer today because they do not seek treatment, heaping misery upon themselves and those that love them.

John Newton reached out to William Cowper. He took him into his household. He encouraged his talents in writing the Olney hymns and engaged his assistance in the fight against slavery. "O for a Closer Walk with God" is a lasting benefit to us from the Newton-Cowper partnership.

We all have a chronic condition, sin. If left untreated, it results in death and eternal separation from God. But there is a permanent cure.

Jesus, the great physician, said, "Come to me, all you that are weary and are carrying heavy burdens, and I will give you rest." (Matthew 11:28)

Re-read the key lyrics of Cowper's hymn. Do you think he found ultimate peace and rest? Do you need to find the purer light that marks the road that leads you to the Lamb?

Prayer
O God of Serenity and Light,

Thank you for your promise of peace and rest in Jesus. Sharpen my vision so that I may see and follow the road that leads me to you. Enlarge my focus so that I may notice and enable others who need my help and encouragement.

In Jesus' Name,
Amen

Resources - http://faithmusicconnection.com/story49

Story # 50
Jesus, the Very Thought of Thee

Story of the Hymn

This is a story of a hymn that might never have been written. Against all odds, "Jesus, the Very Thought of Thee" took over 800 years to make its way into modern hymnals.

Although not unanimous, both Catholic and non-Catholic hymn scholars attribute authorship of "Jesu, dulcis memoria" ("Jesus, Sweet Remembrance,") to St. Bernard of Clairvaux (c. 1090-1153). The original poem of over fifty stanzas reflects the deep faith of the author and is the source of "Jesus, the Very Thought of Thee."

A contemplative man of prayer, Bernard wrote several long poetic and theological works on the nature, life and passion of Jesus Christ. Translations of these works have provided several hymns now sung in English. These include, "O Sacred Head Now Wounded" and "Jesus, Thou Joy of Loving Hearts."

Edward Caswall (1814-1878) translated Bernard's "Jesu, dulcis memoria" into English in 1849. Son of an Anglican priest, Caswall was an honor graduate of Brasenose College, Oxford.

He was ordained in the Church of England in 1840. Like many others, Caswall desired a return to greater piety and formality of liturgy within the church. These ideals became known as the Oxford Movement. Caswall switched to Roman Catholicism in 1847 and was ordained a Catholic priest in 1852.

Following the death of his wife, Caswall began translating many Latin texts into English, including those of St. Bernard. He first published "Jesus, the Very Thought of Thee" in "Lyra Catholica," in London, in 1849. It is, perhaps, the most widely sung of his translations, which also include "When Morning Gilds the Skies."

John Baccus Dykes (1823-1876) composed the tune "St. Agnes" specifically for "Jesus the Very Thought of Thee." Dykes published over 300 hymn tunes, including "Melita," which is associated with the sailors' hymn, "Eternal Father, Strong to Save."

Other Dykes tunes include, "Nicea," the favorite tune universally paired with "Holy, Holy, Holy!" "St. Agnes," "Melita" and "Nicea" represent some of the finest examples of Victorian hymn tunes.

Marked with rich harmonies and melodies in accord with popular music of the day, these tunes encouraged renewed congregational singing.

Key Lyrics

Jesus, the very thought of Thee
With sweetness fills the breast;
But sweeter far Thy face to see,
And in Thy presence rest.

Nor voice can sing, nor heart can frame,
Nor can the memory find
A sweeter sound than Thy blest name,
O Savior of mankind!

Jesus, our only joy be Thou,
As Thou our prize will be;

Jesus be Thou our glory now,
And through eternity.

Devotional – The Test of Time
(I pray) that Christ may dwell in your hearts through faith, as you are being rooted and grounded in love. I pray that you may have the power to comprehend, with all the saints, what is the breadth and length and height and dept, and to know the love of Christ that surpasses knowledge, so that you may be filled with all the fullness of God – Ephesians 3:17-19

Have you ever wondered how the Bible stood the test of time for thousands of years? Consider "Jesus, the Very Thought of Thee." This hymn is a brilliant example of one work that took three people over 800 years to bring to life. Why is this helpful for you to know?

Think back in your life to the times you may have struggled with a challenge or situation where you felt God was not working or moving. It's in these times you may forget that Jesus is a loving God who cares deeply about you and your situation.

Take a moment and review the key lyrics. Do you see God's love for you there? Can you connect to the joy and gratitude that the hymn writer expressed for Jesus?

Jesus is waiting for you and he wants you. How can you express your gratitude or appreciation for him?

Prayer
God and Father, Jesus Christ,

Thank you for making yourself known to me through your Holy Spirit, your word and the witness of believers and seekers through the ages. Scatter the darkness of my night. Inflame my heart with love so that I may seek you more. Make my life a joyful song that reflects your love to all.

In the Name of Jesus,
Amen

Resources - http://faithmusicconnection.com/story50

Story # 51
God of Grace and God of Glory

Story of the Hymn

Did you know the pastor to the powerful industrialist John D. Rockefeller, Jr. wrote a great hymn? And that he was featured on the cover of Time Magazine?

Harry Emerson Fosdick (1878-1969), author of "God of Grace and God of Glory," was one of the most controversial and influential ministers of the twentieth century.

Ordained a Baptist minister, Fosdick served as pastor of First Baptist Church, Montclair, New Jersey, from 1904 to 1915. During this period, he also taught homiletics (preaching) at Union Seminary from 1908 to 1915. Then, he served as professor of homiletics and practical theology there from 1915 until retirement in 1946.

In 1919, Fosdick became associate pastor of Manhattan's First Presbyterian Church. During this pastorate, he preached his famous sermon, "Shall the Fundamentalists Win?" In this homily, he stated his liberal views advocating the inclusion of modern Christians who doubted the literal interpretation of the Bible.

Fosdick's publicist sent copies to churches across the country, not surprisingly stirring up great controversy among Fundamentalists and traditionalists. Ultimately, this led to his resignation from his Presbyterian pastorate in 1925.

The next year, Fosdick accepted an appointment as pastor of Park Avenue Baptist Church. Among its members was the powerful industrialist and philanthropist John D. Rockefeller, Jr. Rockefeller embraced Fosdick's ideals of a ministry inclusive of all races and social classes. It was to this end that he built the interdenominational Riverside Church in the Morningside area of upper Manhattan overlooking the Hudson River.

The Park Avenue congregation and Fosdick moved to this new location. He wrote "God of Grace and God of Glory" for the dedication of the new church in 1931. It was published the next year in a collection entitled, "Praise and Service" and has enjoyed increasing popularity to the present. Fosdick served the church as pastor from its dedication in 1931 until his retirement in 1946.

Key Lyrics
God of grace and God of glory,
On Thy people pour Thy power.
Crown Thine ancient church's story,
Bring her bud to glorious flower.
Grant us wisdom, grant us courage,
For the facing of this hour.

Save us from weak resignation,
To the evils we deplore.
Let the search for Thy salvation,
Be our glory evermore.
Grant us wisdom, grant us courage,
Serving Thee whom we adore.

Devotional – Not a Cosmic Bellboy

"I hereby command you; be strong and courageous; do not be frightened or dismayed, for the Lord your God is with you wherever you go." – Joshua 1:9

Some notable quotations of Harry Emerson Fosdick provide insight into his widespread influence as scholar, teacher and preacher. Consider a few of these for meditation.

"Hating people is like burning down your own house to get rid of a rat."
"Bitterness imprisons life; love releases it."
"It is by acts and not by ideas that people live."

"God is not a cosmic bellboy for whom we can press a button to get things."
"Our power is not so much in us as through us."
"Preaching is personal counseling on a group basis."

"God has put within our lives meanings and possibilities that quite outrun the limits of mortality."

"I would rather live in a world where my life is surrounded by mystery than live in a world so small that my mind could comprehend it."

"The steady discipline of intimate friendship with Jesus results in (people) becoming like Him."

And finally, "Religion is not a burden, not a weight; it is wings."

Prayer
Almighty God,

I am in awe at your infinite power and at the mystery of your love for me. Forgive me for praying to you as if you are a cosmic bellboy ready to provide room service. Give me the humility and wisdom to fulfill your command to be strong and courageous. Raise my awareness of your intimate presence so that your power to love and serve may flow through me.

In Jesus' Name,
Amen

Resources **-** http://faithmusicconnection.com/story51

Story # 52
Great Is Thy Faithfulness

Story of the Hymn

The author of one of the most popular hymns of the 20th century had only an elementary school education. And he spent 44 years of his life as a successful life insurance salesman!

Thomas Obadiah Chisholm (1866-1960), author of "Great Is Thy Faithfulness," had no formal education beyond the eighth grade. His local school in Simpson County, Kentucky, included only eight grades. But Chisholm was a precocious student. Without the benefit of a high-school education, he became the teacher of this one-room country school at age 16. Chisholm also worked for a local weekly newspaper. By the age of 21, he had become associate editor.

In 1893, he had a conversion experience after attending a service conducted by Dr. H. C. Morrison, prominent Methodist evangelist. Dr. Morrison was impressed with the young Chisholm. Later that year, he hired him as managing editor of his publication, "The Pentecostal Herald," in Louisville, Kentucky.

Chisholm was successful in this new position. Soon, his personal faith deepened to the point he felt called to full-time service as a Methodist minister. Ordained in 1903, he was assigned a pastorate at Scottsville, Kentucky, just twenty miles from his birthplace near Franklin.

Failing health cut short this ministry after only a year. He moved with his family to a farm near Winona Lake, Indiana. Winona Lake was the home of the summer Winona Lake Bible Conference. This conference attracted notable personalities in the fields of business, politics and entertainment.

Chisholm's health never recovered to the point that he could take on another pastorate. In 1909, at age 43, he took up a new career as a life insurance salesman. He moved to Vineland, New Jersey, in 1916. There, he successfully continued in life insurance until retirement at age 87 in 1953. Following retirement, he spent the remaining years of his life in a Methodist home for the elderly in Ocean Grove, New Jersey. He died in 1960, at the age of 93.

Today, Chisholm is particularly remembered for two hymns—"Living for Jesus" and "Great is Thy Faithfulness." Undoubtedly, the latter is the most widely popular of his over 800 poetic works. He proclaimed he wrote it as an expression of his deep appreciation to God for the "wonderful displays of His providing care."

Key Lyrics
Great is Thy faithfulness, O God my Father,
There is no shadow of turning with Thee;
Thou changest not, Thy compassions, they fail not;
As Thou hast been, Thou forever will be.

Refrain: Great is Thy faithfulness! Great is Thy faithfulness!
Morning by morning, new mercies I see;
All I have needed, Thy hand hath provided;
Great is Thy faithfulness, Lord, unto me!

Devotional – You Never Know What God Has in Store for You

The steadfast love of the Lord never ceases, his mercies never come to an end; they are new every morning; great is your faithfulness. "The Lord is my portion," says my soul, "therefore I will hope in him." – Lamentations 3:22-24

No matter where you find yourself right now, know this…our God is great in his faithfulness toward you. God used a humble man like Thomas Chisholm to write a powerful hymn that would be sung decades after his death. Imagine what this same God is waiting to do with you.

Thomas O. Chisholm must have been familiar with the above verses from Lamentations as he crafted the lines of his hymn. "Great is Thy Faithfulness" becomes both title and refrain. Other lines of verse in this hymn seem to make direct reference or paraphrase of James 1:17, Hebrews 10:23 and Philippians 4:19-20.

For meditation, read these scriptures and then re-read the key lyrics of the hymn. Chisolm captures the spirit and meaning of these verses without preaching to us. He seems to simply share what he has discovered and lived out in his own life.

Consider Chisolm's long life and the key lyrics of his hymn. Do you think he was happy and content? Why?

Do you see the faithfulness of God in your life?

Are you thankful?

How do you show it?

Prayer
Faithful God, my Father,

Thank you for your faithfulness and gracious provision for all my needs. Forgive me for taking blessings and opportunities for granted. Increase my faith so that I may be more aware of your faithfulness and more eager to live as your faithful servant.

In Jesus' Name,
Amen

Resources - http://faithmusicconnection.com/story52

Alphabetical Index by Hymn Title

About the Author

Dr. Larry Frazier

Larry and his wife Mary Lynn were particularly inspired, strengthened and encouraged by the power of the stories behind great hymns during her battle with cancer over ten years ago. During this trying time of surgery and chemotherapy treatments, Larry launched his radio program, "The Hymn of the Week," which has reached and continues to inspire hundreds of thousands of listeners in West Georgia, Alabama and Tennessee. The stories behind the creation of these great hymns inspired him to write, "A Story Behind Every Hymn: 52 Weeks of Inspiration, Courage and Strength."

Larry attends Carrollton First Baptist Church where he is a soloist, choir member, adult Sunday School teacher and deacon.

His website, www.FaithMusicConnection.com provides complete lyrics, expanded history as well as performances of the hymns in this book.

Additional Resources

We have created additional resource guides that you may be interested in receiving for free as my gift to you.

To claim your gift, please go to:
http://faithmusicconnection.com/book-gifts